FOAL

HATCH, MATCH, AND DISPATCH

HATCH, MATCH, AND DISPATCH

The Life and Times of the *Almost*
Reverend William Billow

REV. WILLIAM BILLOW

Guilford, Connecticut

An imprint of The Rowman & Littlefield Publishing Group, Inc.
4501 Forbes Blvd., Ste. 200
Lanham, MD 20706
www.rowman.com

Distributed by NATIONAL BOOK NETWORK

British Library Cataloguing in Publication Information available

Library of Congress Cataloging-in-Publication Data available

ISBN 978-1-4930-3701-8 (hardcover)
ISBN 978-1-4930-3842-8 (e-book)

♾™ The paper used in this publication meets the minimum requirements of American National
Standard for Information Sciences—Permanence of Paper for Printed Library Materials, ANSI/
NISO Z39.48-1992.

Printed in the United States of America

For Mom

CONTENTS

CONTENTS

Contents

ACKNOWLEDGMENTS

I WISH TO EXPRESS MY THANKS TO THE FOLLOWING PEOPLE: ANN Selinger, my dear friend and assistant for many years, who agreed to take on the daunting task of initial edits. Michael Duffy, a friend and St. Albans dad who early on said, "You've got a book." Jean Becker, chief of staff for President George H. W. Bush. Eric Bryant of Unboxed Productions for his patience and technical expertise. My sisters, Sally Wallace and Kim Armondo, for their memories and brothers-in-law, Larry and Sam, who put up with all the reminiscing. The Reverend Bill Hague, the Reverend Billy Shand, and Nell and Merv Hampton, friends and fellow seminary survivors. Anona Fowler, Sheila Lindveit, Karen Fitzgerald, and Louise Lusignan, the combined heart of St. Columba's. My retirees group from St. Albans—Bryan Leithauser, Paul Barrett, Paul Piazza, Mary Hardman, Linda DeBord, and Sheila Murawski—who listened to stories and encouraged me. Ann Owens, Greg Parker, Joyce Murphy, Lee Sturtevant, Molly Meinhart, Joan Roshkosh, Mark Wilkerson, Robin Boswell, Pam Grant, and, of course, Vance Wilson, who were helpful about all things St. Albans. Walter Thorne, former student and now a chaplain himself, for his sense of humor and his patience. Stephanie Scott, my kind and patient editor at Lyons Press. Production editor Meredith Dias, copy editor Elissa Curcio, cover designer Diana Nuhn, and layout artist Jason Rock. Flossie Fowlkes, LC, for her love and encouragement. And finally for the "communion of saints" who gave me the material.

FOREWORD

I AM NOT SURE WHEN I MET THE GOOD REVEREND WILLIAM BILLOW—
I hope he forgives me if I call him Will henceforth. At age ninety-three
(likely ninety-four by the time you read this), I really can't remember
when I met anyone anymore, except of course for Barbara. But I do know
that Will is one of those special people who have drifted in and out of
our lives for a very long time. And thankfully so.

Over the years, through his pastorship at various churches attended
by the Bush clan, he has brought us great comfort, inspiration, and more
than a few smiles. Like all of our pastors, he's played an important part
of our spiritual journey.

But it's his journey, not mine, that you will take through the pages of
this delightful book. When at age four he stole the Baby Jesus from the
church Nativity scene, you might say he knew he had a calling. It took
him a few more years to figure out exactly what that calling was, but lucky
for those of us whose paths crossed with his, he did.

I must say I learned a lot from this book, including some incidents
involving me. I didn't know, for example, the Secret Service momentarily
feared one Christmas Eve that Mary and Joseph might be terrorists. Or
that one of my relatives drove into an open grave on the day of Uncle
Lou's funeral.

But enough of revealing what is in the pages ahead. I will leave to you
the joy of reading the ups and downs of the story of one very special priest.

One last note to our friend Will: I've had the privilege of writing
numerous forewords over the years. The title of this book is, with very little competition, my favorite. You will have fun figuring out what it means.

—George H. W. Bush

INTRODUCTION

I WAS TALKED INTO WRITING THIS BOOK BY ITS PUBLISHER, JED LYONS. He is a great friend. His sons were my students at St. Albans, and he and his wife, Blythe, have probably sat through as many of my homilies at weddings, baptisms, and funerals as anyone. Hence *Hatch, Match, and Dispatch*. It is an expression I once heard that describes the job of being a minister or priest or whatever you want to call what I am. Jed told me this book would be a labor of love, and that it has been.

For those of you who might not know, the Episcopal Church is big on titles. The late, great Bishop of Washington, John Thomas Walker, once said he thought I would one day be a bishop. Bishops are known as *right* reverends, cathedral deans as *very* reverends, and archbishops as *most* reverends. People are always asking me about the proper way to refer to me. I actually just prefer "Will." I never made it to the exalted position of bishop, but if we have to ascribe a title, I think "The *Almost* Reverend" suits me just fine.

I Know My Own and
My Own Know Me

IF I AM TO THINK OF A BIBLE PASSAGE THAT WOULD SUM UP MY MINIS-
try, I hope it would be the passage above from the tenth chapter of the
Gospel of John. It is the passage where Jesus is describing the Good
Shepherd's relationship to the sheep. Being a priest is likened to being a
shepherd. People do, from time to time, need a poke here or a prod there.
But mostly, they need to know someone is watching out for them.

Since ordination to the priesthood, I must confess I have never been
much interested in books that talk about the "study and practice" of ministry. The most effective advice for me was *just do it*. Just show up. Just be
there. Just listen. Some theologian coined it "the ministry of presence."

I remember a professor and advisor in seminary who taught pastoral
theology. Mostly, he talked about creating "boundaries." He was confrontational. He actually had all of us scared to call him about anything.
You're *never* to just drop in. *Always* make appointments. Not exactly the
way you want your parishioners, particularly students, to feel about you. I
did *not* follow his advice. My office at St. Albans operated like a drop-in
center.

That particular professor had a lousy relationship with the students.
Later, I heard he actually went into parish ministry and I wondered about
those poor parishioners.

I have to confess creating "boundaries" has never been my strong
suit—my parishioners, colleagues, and students have become my *friends*.

I

I, of course, have grown to understand boundaries and appropriate behavior because I had sage advice from my mentors along the way. But friendship goes both ways. My students and parishioners befriended *me* in spite of my shortcomings. For example, I recently read back over some of my sermons and thought, "Oh no, those poor people actually had to listen to that!"

A little later in the fifteenth chapter of John's Gospel, Jesus actually says, "But I have called you friends." Though for me, being a "friend" has meant many missed dinners, phone calls in the middle of the night, and interrupted vacations; more importantly, it has meant the privilege of being with people I love during the most meaningful moments of their lives.

I wouldn't have had it any other way.

That's what "friends" are for, and this one just happens to also be a priest.

A Midwestern Boyhood

THE FOLLOWING CHILDHOOD STORIES DID MUCH TO PREPARE ME FOR the life situations in which my parishioners, students, and friends have found themselves. I used to think my experiences were unique to me, and for a time I was embarrassed by some of them, but over the years I have found there isn't much we all don't have in common. And now most of the things that once embarrassed me make me laugh.

STEALING THE BABY JESUS

My journey to the priesthood began at St. Phillip's Episcopal Church in Palatine, Illinois.

Father Foote was the rector, and he couldn't preach very well. Everyone in the congregation remembered when I, as a little boy, clapped when his sermon was over. But he was loving and kind, and that seemed to be the most important thing.

When I was four, we were having our usual Christmas pageant and Father Foote neglected to choose me to place the figure of baby Jesus in the manger, as he had the year before. I raced up, grabbed the baby Jesus, and ran back to the pew. Not missing a beat, Father Foote said, "Will, would you like to place baby Jesus in the manger?" I nodded yes, and walked back up the aisle and placed him gently in the manger. I assume the service went on without any more major incidents.

I guess that was a harbinger of things to come.

As soon as I was old enough, I became an acolyte and would serve Father Foote at the eight and ten o'clock services. The problem was, I had to kneel for very long stretches of time and would often faint, so I didn't last very long. But at least I didn't throw up during the service like my friend and co-acolyte LeMoine D. Stitt III, also known as "Three," did.

St. Phillip's was what is considered "high" church. The liturgy was chanted, and there was often incense. The services were *always* Communion services.

In later years, I took a hiatus from church, as do many teenagers. But I think during my years as an acolyte, I was deeply affected by the words we hear over and over again in the liturgy, "on the night before He died for us." At a critical moment in my young adult life, those words led to the discovery of an imperfect jewel. After finding it, I became a priest.

BOYHOOD IN THE MIDWEST

My midwestern boyhood began in a small community forty miles outside of Chicago in a place called Inverness.

Inverness had once been a farm owned by Arthur T. MacIntosh, a Chicago real estate developer and family friend, who subdivided it into beautiful home sites surrounding a golf course. There was also a stable with riding trails. Our house at 307 Inverway Road was a pretty Cape Cod and looked out on the 14th hole on one of the highest points of Inverness. Because of our four dogs, Sassy, Bingo, Peg, and Maggie, Dad would describe our house as being "on the corner of Turd Street and Inverway."

Along with the Arthur T. and Gilbert MacIntoshes, our friends and neighbors included original residents of Inverness, all of whom lived along Inverway Road: Stanley and Gracie Pepper, Moine and Mimi Stitt, Emory and Ruthie Moore, Hardy and Jane Hodgson, Mike and Ethel Garry, Carl and Joanie Buehler, Bud and Peppi Grosse, Bob and Peggy Cantwell, Jean and Tom Hicks, Ted and Marian Miller, and Fritz and Peg Rueckert.

The local newspaper had a column called Items from Inverness. The following stories *never* made it into it . . .

When we were little, someone in the neighborhood had a kidnapping threat. When Mom asked Dad if we needed to worry, Dad said, "If someone took our kids, they would soon be paying us to take them back."

My first role. "I Am the Captain of the *Pinafore!*"

AUTHOR'S PERSONAL COLLECTION

Our dog Sassy would steal golf balls from the green behind our house and bring them home. Mom had to hide in the bushes and throw them back.

My sister Kim had a lemonade stand on the golf course. When Dad and his foursome came along, he sent her in to get some vodka, until Mom intervened.

The Rueckerts' dog, Bongo, would steal steaks off the grill at the Inverness Country Club, and Fritz Rueckert would have to reimburse the club.

Dad drove our new Jaguar to the club for a round of golf. Without Dad knowing, the teenage valet drove it into Palatine to show his girlfriend, who worked at the lumber yard. He parked it on some railroad tracks in the yard that he assumed were dormant. A train hit it.

My "Uncle Hardy" Hodgson was the golf club champ, and when he died, his kids buried his ashes in the sand trap behind our house because while he was alive, "he spent a lot of time in it."

The following story can be found in an old pamphlet I found entitled "The History of Inverness Golf Club."

Dad and a few of our neighbors had a regular Saturday afternoon poker group at the Inverness Golf Club. Regular attendees included Dad and several friends.

The club was closed in February, and not wanting to miss four sessions, they had arranged to meet at the Cow Palace on Route 14. On the third Saturday, they were raided by deputies from the sheriff's department. One of them escaped, but got home without his shoes. Hence, he acquired the nickname "Sneakers." An article that appeared in the Sunday *Chicago Tribune* referred to the group as "a number of prominent Palatine businessmen." Mom hid the newspaper from us and didn't let us watch TV for several days.

THE HORSE IN THE KITCHEN

While in Inverness we had a housekeeper, Louise, known as "Wheetee"; a nanny, Betty; a yardman, Vasilly, known as "Be a Silly"; and his wife, Anna, also a housekeeper—all of whom we loved.

Mom had a lot of help. Turns out she would need it.

My two cousins, Elizabeth and Charles, came to live with us for a time after the death of my aunt, Ann Billow, in a car accident on the Pennsylvania Turnpike on May 30, 1952. And then on August 2, 1955, my uncle, John Faller Jr., an attorney, was killed in a shooting in the Cumberland County Courthouse in Carlisle, Pennsylvania. The husband in a divorce case, after being ordered to pay fifty dollars a month in support, shot his estranged wife, Uncle John, the judge, and another lawyer. Uncle John was the only one who died. His son, "young John," came to live with us for a time too.

So did my grandparents when they were widowed.

Oh, and did I mention that we also had four dogs and a horse, and that one day my sister Kim brought her horse, Missy, through the breezeway into the kitchen?

Kim riding Missy

I think that was just too much for Wheetee, who had a nervous breakdown. She would sit in the rocking chair in the nursery and repeat over and over, "Poor, poor Louise . . ."

Dad put her on the train to go back to her family in Chicago.

That might have been when my sister Sally, who was five, told Mom she wanted to run away.

So Mom said, "OK, honey, but you'll need a few things." So Mom brought a suitcase down from the attic and she and Sally packed it with the things she would need for her journey, complete with a lunch for her trip down Inverway Road.

Mom called all the neighbors to tell them Sally was running away, and they all said they would keep an eye out for her. Sally was well known in the neighborhood.

Sally, about the time she ran away

Joan Buehler, who we called "Boodie," loved to tell the story of Sally appearing at the back door, asking if she had a head of lettuce because Mom needed it for dinner. Boodie, who was having a dinner party herself that night, watched as Sally ate it while walking across the golf course toward our house.

When she got to Mimi Stitt's house, she sat down and Mimi watched her eat her lunch. When she was finished, Sally closed up her suitcase and came home. Mom helped her unpack her bag, and she put it back in the attic . . . until the next time.

The Inverness gang

Halloween

On my desk at home, I have a picture of my friends and me at my friend Stevie's birthday party. We're all surrounding his golden retriever, Rex. There in the picture are Stevie, Randy, "Three," Ricky, Charlie, and Rory. Someone behind Charlie is making "rabbit ears" over Ricky's head. I think it's Jaybo.

Everyone is in jeans except for yours truly, who is dressed up like Little Lord Fauntleroy.

It's a sweet picture of little boys who grew up in the country. We played army, built tree forts, and went on "safaris" in the woods behind the houses until our moms called us and it was time to go home.

One of our favorite times was Halloween.

Now before I tell this Halloween story, I want you to know there is *a lot* wrong with it. It involves many things we are now taught *not* to do.

Halloween was a big deal in Inverness. We'd start at one end of Inverway Road. There were seventeen houses, and we'd hit them all. One of our parents would have to drive because it was too far to walk. We would always end up at Marian Miller's house. She always dressed up like a witch. She also had a life-size wolf in sheep's clothing on her exercise machine, and when you flipped the switch, it would look like the wolf was exercising!

One particular year it was "Aunt" Peg's turn to drive us. She had an enormous station wagon with a "way-back." We would all pile in. There were no such things as seat belts then, and at every stop Aunt Peg would have a cocktail with the neighbors while we were getting our candy.

Anyway, we arrived safely at Marian's and we all flew inside to see the wolf—except for someone Aunt Peg could see in the rearview mirror.

She asked, "What's the matter, honey? Aren't you going on to get some candy?"

No answer. She turned around. It was her black Lab.

These are the things I "prefer" to remember: the fun and the laughter.

Lest I romanticize, as the Chinese proverb states, "If I accept the sunshine and warmth, I must also accept the thunder and lightning."

Aunt Peg died of cancer not long after that Halloween.

As I gaze at that picture on my desk—at each individual life—it will not surprise you that in it, along with the joy of that particular moment in time, I can also see heartbreak that, too, can come with the years.

In that photograph, I see alcoholism, suicide, depression, divorce—but I also see people who loved and were loved, and parents who tried their best.

REVISING YOUR MAP

In recent years I became reacquainted with a daughter of my dad's best friend.

Her father was a top executive with a major company in Chicago. He was an extraordinarily talented painter and an avid sportsman. During the course of our childhood, alcoholism overtook him: He was passed over for a promotion. He would disappear for days on end. He shot out the windows of their home with a shotgun. At one point my dad found him passed out in a flophouse in downtown Chicago with several hundred thousand dollars' worth of stock certificates strewn across the floor. At that same time, this particular daughter was diagnosed with cancer, from which she recovered.

Things ended badly with her family. Her parents divorced, and she had very little to do with her father after that. He died soon after. Her mother moved away, and we saw very little of the family. She did not have happy memories of her father, and when she did speak of him, she was very critical.

Years later while I was visiting my dad and his wife, Dorane, in Seattle, she came for dinner and very pointedly asked them about her father, and what they thought brought about his downfall. Their response was simply, "You! It was out of worry for you." Clearly shocked, she fell silent. It was her reaction that most surprised me: It appeared that thought had never occurred to her that her illness might have affected her father in such a way. Of course, the reasons for a person's falling into alcoholism are many and varied, genetics having a great deal to do with it. After he became sober in his later years, my own father warned me to "watch out." There can be a slow and steady decline with no apparent tipping point, but some alcoholics I have known have spoken of a singular event that pushed them over the edge.

Whether or not that was the case in this situation, I have wondered how the response to her question might have altered her opinion of her father. Children and adults are often surprised when they are confronted with new information. The late author and psychologist Scott Peck, a friend of mine and author of the best-selling books *The Road Less Traveled* and *People of the Lie*, would say, "We are given a map with which we negotiate the terrain of life, and from time to time the map needs to be revised."

I wonder if she revised hers.

STRIP POKER

Dee Dee Weeks was my best girl "friend." The Weekses were neighbors in Inverness. They lived in the original MacIntosh farmhouse, and as kids we spent a lot of time there. My sister Kim had a crush on Dee Dee's brother Cappy, so she'd ride her horse over there every chance she got.

Charlotte Weeks, Dee Dee's mother, was a Lunken. The Lunkens had donated the land that became Lunken Airfield in Cincinnati, which at that time was the largest airfield in the United States. When the airfield was dedicated, attendees included Howard Hughes and Jean Harlow. Charles Lindbergh would refuel his plane there when flying to and from New York. I remember meeting the Hollywood director Sid Luft at their house. At the time, he was married to Judy Garland, who played Dorothy in *The Wizard of Oz*.

One day in the late afternoon, while our mothers were having cocktails, we were playing cards with Candy, Dee Dee's best friend, and someone suggested we play strip poker.

If you've never played, everyone lays a card down and low card loses. If you have the low card, you have to take off an article of clothing. I was at a definite disadvantage because the girls had figured out that if they were wearing curlers (which they were), they could take one out every time they lost.

For whatever reason, the mothers got suspicious and our game was interrupted. After that there were no more "sleepovers" at our houses with girls.

MEET STUPID

When I was ten years old, I learned I had a half brother and sister. I'm not sure when Mom and Dad intended to tell us.

My sister Sally learned quite by accident when she was out visiting Dad and his fourth wife, Dorane. The phone rang and Sally answered it, and a young male voice asked to speak to his dad. Sally told him he had the wrong number, and he clarified, "Mr. Billow." The cat was out of the bag.

Mom once told me when they married for the *second* time that she knew about a marriage in between and the one child. She said she didn't know about the other.

Dad was a Phi Beta Kappa graduate of Dickinson College, and he could be clever and charming. He became a very successful businessman whose employees loved him, but he was an alcoholic with a mercurial temper when drinking. He also had a wandering eye.

"Nancy, why in the world did you marry Bill Billow again?"

When he met Mom, he was a manager of the Statler Hotel in Cleveland. Mom was twenty, beautiful, bright, and living at home in Painesville, Ohio. She was an honors graduate of the King-Smith finishing school in Washington, DC, where she had studied dance with Martha Graham.

They married, the war came along, and Dad went to Officer Candidate School. He graduated a "ninety-day wonder" in the navy and was posted to San Diego. There they had my sister Kim. A couple of years later, they were posted to Seattle, where he was the chief commissary officer at Sand Point. My sister Sally was born. Soon after came the first divorce.

Mom moved back to Ohio with the girls. They lived in a cottage on my grandparents' property on Lake Erie, where Mom had a stint as cohost of a television show. A story my grandmother told was that Sally, as a little girl, would hit the TV because she couldn't understand why Mom wouldn't answer her.

Much to the dismay of my grandparents, Mom and Dad married again, and shortly thereafter I was born and we moved to Inverness, where Dad took a job selling lumber at a company owned by Jack Fiddes and my godfather, Emory Moore.

For a time those were happy years on Inverway Road, until the drinking and womanizing took their toll. One evening Mom was walking through the den and heard Dad whispering into the phone, "I'll meet you tomorrow night." When he put the phone down, Mom said, "Why don't you just go tonight."

Many years later at dinner one evening, Betty Martin, a great friend of Mom's, asked, "Why in the world did you marry Bill Billow again? That was stupid." Mom pointed at me and said, "Meet stupid."

CHARLIE AND KELLY

After the initial shock of learning I had a half brother and sister, my curiosity about them was satisfied when on my next trip out to Seattle, I met them. At some point their home life became difficult, and Dad found it necessary to intervene in their upbringing. For a time Charlie went to live with Dad and Dorane, and Kelly went to live in Canada with close friends. I am unaware of the circumstances that led to Dad's intervention. I only know that during a speech he gave several years ago in Seattle, Charlie spoke of relying on food stamps to live. Whatever it was that occurred in their childhood, they had and continue to have very loving and supportive relationships with their half siblings.

I think we had little to do with them when we were young because of reluctance on my mother's part. As we grew older and care of Dad and Dorane became more complicated, we grew to be good friends.

Having started selling produce from a truck on the side of the road, Charlie is now the largest produce distributor on the West Coast, with delivery trucks bearing the name "Charlie's Produce" from Alaska to California. Because of his experience as a child, Charlie and his wife, Courtni, are ardent supporters of Food Lifeline in Seattle and Charlie's trucks deliver his produce to over 275 food banks.

Kelly remained in Canada, where she and her husband, Edward, became social workers. I officiated at the baptisms of Kelly's three sons and at the wedding of Charlie's daughter Brittany—and sadly, also at Kelly's funeral. She passed away in 2016 after having been diagnosed with a rare form of brain cancer.

If It Hadn't Been for Your Mother

Dorane was Dad's secretary and the woman to whom he was whispering on the phone. She moved with him to Seattle after Mom and Dad's second and final divorce.

Dad had pleaded with Mom not to divorce again. Mom said she felt she had no choice, with him behaving as he did. She once said, "It wasn't the other women, it was the drinking. Your father had an explosive temper, and I couldn't raise you kids in an environment like that." She did, however, let my sisters and me fly out to Seattle every year in the summer to spend a month with Dad and Dorane, where we witnessed that sort

Dad and Dorane

of behavior firsthand. It was only bad in the evenings after cocktail hour and during dinner.

We did have some great times. Living on Lake Washington, we learned to sail and water-ski, and we would take trips together exploring the Pacific Northwest. However, on one particular camping trip, my sister Sally heard Dorane crying in the middle of the night in the tent next door. Having a tearful conversation with Dad, she kept repeating, "You promised you'd marry me."

Sally, being twelve years old, immediately recounted what she overheard when we got back home to Illinois. Mom called Dad and said that this was unacceptable, and we would not be coming back out unless he resolved the situation. A few days later Dad called back and said to Mom, "Well, it's your fault! I married her."

Dorane, devoted to Dad, found herself in a role as stepmother to five children, from Dad's two previous marriages. I loved Dorane, although she could be direct and difficult. With all due respect, she tried hard to make us into some semblance of a family—her family—and was devoted to us. When we would visit, she took off work and spent all her time with us. She would arrange dinners with Charlie and Kelly so we could get to know them.

When we were young, Dad would spend every Christmas with us in Illinois, and Dorane would go to her parents' farm in South Dakota. While in Seattle, Dad had a very different social life than the life he led in Inverness. The drinking made him reclusive. Never wanting to have a house again, Dad bought a condo in Madison Park on Lake Washington in Seattle, and he and Dorane spent most of their time together—their shared interests being work, hunting, and golf. They had few close friends. As the years went by, they grew more and more isolated and dependent on one another. At about age seventy, Dad did quit drinking, although Dorane did not.

When I transferred to the University of Washington my third year of college, I would have dinner with them once a week (watching Lawrence Welk!), and we remained in close touch. When Dad became ill, he asked me if I would please watch out for Dorane. I kept that promise, although after Dad died she began losing what "filter" she had, and what she said could be hurtful.

Upon her death, she divided her trust equally among all of us kids. Not long before she died, she confessed, "I'm not sure your father ever really loved me." I think she believed as I do—Mom was the love of his life. I never told her of something I was aware Dad had said to Mom many years earlier: "Sweetie, if it's Dorane, I'll get rid of her tomorrow."

Mom and Dorane had a respectful relationship. I think they each taught me how to make the best out of relationships in a divorce. Mom once said, "I'm fond of Dorane, and I think we would have been good friends if circumstances had been different." In a similar generous moment, Dorane said to me, "This never would have worked if it had not been for your mother."

WHEN THE ROOF FALLS IN

I want to be fair about my dad. He loved me and I loved him. Even though he was a self-professed atheist, he was very proud of me and the success I had achieved. It was well known in his family that as a young man, he had an interest in theology and even taught Sunday school. My grandmother held out hope that he would someday become a minister. That calling would fall to her grandson.

Dad's alcoholism caused a lot of problems for our family. Once while driving drunk on Christmas Eve, he crashed into a car being driven by the Palatine fire chief, who was delivering fruit baskets. Pineapples, apples, and oranges ended up all over Route 14. Luckily no one was seriously hurt. On a humorous note, every year following he got a Christmas card from the chief.

He always had the best interests of his children at heart. As a little girl, my sister Kim had two make-believe friends named Ghee and Gerr. They were twins. Mom would even set places at the table for them at Kim's insistence. Once while on a family trip to Seattle, we were in a hurry to get to the airport and raced to get into a cab outside the Olympic Hotel. When we got to the end of the block, Kim started to scream, "We left Ghee on the steps!" Not wanting to do irreparable psychological damage to his child, Dad insisted the driver go around the block and let Ghee in the car. The driver totally understood and said "I have kids too." My make-believe friend was Mrs. Heehaw. To the best of my knowledge, Sally never had one.

In spite of his alcoholism, Dad became very successful in the lumber business, becoming chairman of Brady International Lumber Company, a Seattle wholesaler for whom he began to work after he and Dorane moved to Seattle. After his divorce from Mom, he never again drank during the day, only after work, so as not to affect the business, though this was not so great for his family life. He would usually stop at Broadmoor Golf Club on the way home from work and have a "couple of pops" with friends.

The evening would deteriorate from there. Dinners were difficult. He could be demeaning and critical. There was no sense in arguing a point because you could never win.

When he was sober, he was great. He was dependable, trustworthy, honest, and kind. He was generous with his children, and believing strongly in education, put us through college and graduate school. After he died, his business associates and friends told me of loans he had made, many of which he had forgiven. There is a company story told of a contract he made with simply a handshake. When the agreement wasn't honored by the other party, Dad did take it to court, but when he learned the defendant would have to go into bankruptcy, Dad forgave the loan.

Dad was clever and quick-witted. One funny story is told by Casey Knowles, a Vietnam veteran and close family friend, who Dad hired after his tour of duty. After a while, unhappy with his salary, Casey went in to see Dad and said, "Bill, garbage men in Seattle make more money than I do." Dad replied, "Casey, do you want to *be* a garbage man?"

Casey ended up owning the company.

Dad was very private about his personal life. Perhaps he was embarrassed or he really believed it wasn't anyone's business but his own. As an adult, I had become aware he had been married in college to a woman whose family owned the Molly Pitcher Hotel in Carlisle, Pennsylvania. A friend of mine had read of the marriage in a Dickinson College alumni bulletin and asked if it was my dad. A few years later, on the way to play golf at Broadmoor, I asked him about it. He slammed on the brakes and looking straight ahead said, "That is none of your goddamn business!" Nothing more was said, and we continued on to the club.

The sober Dad is the one I now wish to remember—the scratch golfer who taught me to play golf, fish, and hunt. The Dad who got up every morning at four and, smoking cigarette after cigarette, read the *Atlantic Monthly* and the *New Yorker* from cover to cover. The Dad who could quote Shakespeare and E. E. Cummings, and the Bible. The Dad who loved Louis Armstrong and whose favorite song was the Beatles' "Let It Be." The Dad who purposely left a *Playboy* in the backseat of the car so I would find it. The Dad who hunted in Idaho with Ernest Hemingway, whom he thought was a "horse's kertoodle" (rear end). The Dad who brought Bing Crosby home for breakfast during a golf tournament and didn't wake my sister Sally up to meet him. (Sally's never gotten over it.) The Dad who left his children original sculptures by Henry Moore and Jean Arp and paintings by Mark Tobey and Milton Avery.

Dad mellowed a lot with age, particularly after he quit drinking. In a reflective moment late in life, he once said to me, "Your mother and I should never have gotten divorced." When I told Mom what he had said, she replied, "Well maybe *he* didn't think so."

I sometimes wonder if Dad might really have been an agnostic. After I was ordained, he flew me home to give Communion to a family friend who was dying of cancer. He also had me to lunch with several of his Broadmoor golf buddies, who told me they'd invest in me if I'd become a TV evangelist because "there's big money in it!"

A lifelong Republican, he voted his conscience. He was a firm believer in civil rights, and while we were watching a basketball game at Broadmoor with several club members, he asked me to be excused for a moment and then excoriated them for using racial slurs with me in the room. He also hired our nanny Betty Nomura immediately following the Japanese internment during World War II.

After coming home from church one Sunday morning, I sat down to have lunch with Dad, and he looked at me and said, "I thought of going to church with you this morning, but I didn't think it would be fair to the rest of the people when I walked in the door and the roof fell in."

That is a risk I would have happily taken.

FAMILY SECRETS

While growing up, I didn't know much about the Billows. After some research I discovered they were from Carlisle, Pennsylvania. Peter Casper von Bulow, my first Billow ancestor in America, was a Hessian soldier who fought for the British during the Revolutionary War. He married a woman who was Cherokee. He was imprisoned in Carlisle, and after his release he became a farmer in Perry County. There was a historic covered bridge in Dellville known as "Billow's Bridge." Sadly, an arsonist burned it down several years ago.

Mom's side of the family, the Kimballs, are from Madison, Ohio. I have more stuff from them, including my great-great-grandfather's campaign chest and sword and my great-grandmother's silver. We have a coat of arms. Through Richard Kimball and his offspring, I qualify to be a Son of the American Revolution. But there was a bit of a mystery surrounding one ancestor in particular.

Last year I learned my great-grandfather had been murdered. His name was George Mayo.

I knew that my grandmother Helen, whom we called Nana, had been raised by her grandparents, of whom she was very proud. Her grandfather, Judge Henry Mayo, became postmaster of Ottawa, Illinois. He married Isabella Kistler, whose family had a farm just outside of Ottawa. Judge Mayo's portrait hangs in the courthouse, and he is often referred to in histories of Ottawa. Mayo's Island in the middle of the Illinois River in downtown Ottawa is named for him.

I still don't know why Nana was raised by her grandparents. When I asked Mom, she was rather vague. I'm not sure she knew. Mom was an only child and *thought* she was the only grandchild on both sides of the family. As it turns out, she was not.

If I am to believe the research I've gleaned from newspaper accounts, Henry and Isabella Mayo had six children, one of whom was named George. He grew up in Ottawa and married a woman named Maude Jerome. They had five children, one of whom was Nana. George was what was known as a "springtime farmer" and was murdered in a fight in an onion field in Lee Township, Michigan, in 1932. The stepson of Harry Blauvelt, the owner of the onion field, reportedly hit George in the head with a club because he was threatening him with a knife. According to the paper, the case was dismissed by the judge and all charges were dropped.

At the time of the murder, Nana was already married to my grandfather, Park Kimball, and had an eleven-year-old daughter, my mom, Nancy. To the best of my knowledge, they never spoke of it, or if they did, they kept the information vaulted from the children and grandchildren.

It remains one of the many things I will now never know that give me pause. But I guess theirs was a generation that didn't speak of such things.

FATHER FOOTE

I think the retelling of this story in the family gave me a wide-eyed perspective on clergy, church doctrine, and having one's own mind about it all. Like several stories in this book, it *shouldn't* be told from the pulpit. It is written with thanks to Dottie Kimball, my step-grandmother.

As a kid, I went to St. Phillips Church in Palatine, Illinois. Fiddes and Moore, the company for whom Dad worked, donated the lumber for the church, so to many of the folks in Inverness, it was also referred to as St. Fiddes and Moore.

Father Foote was the rector. He had a dog named Nebuchadnezzar, or "Nebbie" for short, named for the biblical king in the Old Testament. When my folks divorced, Father Foote spent a lot of time with our family and we all loved him. Well, almost all of us.

Enter Dottie Kimball. Dottie had married Mom's father, Park Kimball, after Nana's death. Nana and Park, whom we called Parkie, lived in Painesville, Ohio, for many years before they retired to their home in Madison-on-the-Lake. Nana's death was totally unexpected. When Parkie married Dottie relatively soon after, it was a bit of a shock. Dottie was *very* different from my grandmother. Nana Kimball was *very* refined, but Dottie was a diamond in the rough. And she loved her cocktails, which probably led to the incident I'm about to tell.

A couple of years after my folks' divorce, Mom met George Heppe, the man who would become her next husband. When they decided to marry, they asked Father Foote to officiate. However, at that time

Kim, Jaybo Buehler, and me. Can you find Jaybo?

Parkie, Dottie, Sally, Kim, and me at Mom and George's wedding

divorced Episcopalians were not allowed to be remarried in the church, and Father Foote was not able to officiate at the ceremony. Well, let's just say this did not sit well with Dottie Kimball. Never mind church doctrine. She was furious with Father Foote.

She was visiting us when he came to dinner one evening. She was perfectly charming during dinner, but when Father Foote left, Dottie put down her drink, looked at Mom, and said, "Well, if you want to know what I think, I think Father *Prick* . . . is a *foot*!"

To give you a little more of an idea about Dottie Kimball, the night she met my brother-in-law Larry, she was sitting on a green velvet settee in the living room. When he walked in the door, Dottie, with a drink in one hand and a cigarette in the other, said, "Hey, honey! I didn't think I was going to like you because you're Italian and Roman Catholic, but just come over here and sit on grandma's lap."

I FOUND YOU JUST IN TIME

George C. Heppe was known as *the* bachelor on the Gold Coast of Chicago until at forty-seven he married Mom. His father, George H. Heppe, was in the meat-packing business, had a seat on the Chicago Board of Trade, and owned the Seneca Hotel. The family had a home on Lake Geneva, Wisconsin. George worked at the hotel during summers and called it the "Sneaka Hotel" because businessmen would sneak in at lunchtime with women other than their wives.

Mom and George met at a party in Inverness given by John and Betty Kellogg Goodwillie. Someone smashed in the door of Mom's car parked on the side of Baldwin Road, and George drove her home. She said she thought at first that he was a gigolo.

We moved to Palatine, the closest town to Inverness, after Mom and George married. Now that we were older, only Anna and "Be a Silly" came with us, and we lived in a pretty white colonial house on Smith Street. Mom was angry with Roy LaLonde, the Realtor, because he brought her in "the other way" and neglected to tell her the dump was at the end of our street. Hence, it was known by all as "444 North Smith Street, between the cemetery and the dump." When they came to see us, the Buehlers used to hold their breath when they drove by the cemetery.

I found you "just in time."

Mom, George, Sally, and me at Brookfield Zoo, Chicago

George with me in my very favorite Halloween costume

George was a kind and loving stepfather. He was a steadying influence compared to my dad's issues with alcoholism and how that affected our family. He helped me with my homework. He taught me to ride a bike. He also bought me a car for graduation from high school because his father had done the same for him. His was a Packard. Mine was a blue 1968 Camaro 327 convertible I wish I still had.

I never heard him say a bad word about anyone. His favorite song was "Just in Time" because that's the way he felt about meeting Mom.

His mother lived with us for a time. She was extremely difficult and very jealous of Mom, as she had lived with George until his marriage. Mom said, "She thought I stole her husband." One day Mom came home and found my sisters crying on the front steps of the house because of something "Grandma" Heppe had said or done. That was the last straw. Mom said to George, "It's either your mother or me." The next week Grandma Heppe was on a train to go live with George's sister in Arizona.

George introduced us "hicks from the sticks" to Chicago society. His best friend from childhood was C. D. "Chuck" Peacock III. The Peacocks owned a jewelry store on Michigan Avenue, and George would bring me with him when he went down to "Chuck's store." Their pals were the Val Christmans, the Henry Iserts, the Carl Wittbolts, and the Lee Jacobses. The Jacobses' daughter, Jamee, married Marshall Field V. As a young boy, I remember going to the Ringlings' estate in Sarasota, and George told me about the acrobats that performed at their parties when he was a boy.

He was a member of two exclusive clubs in Chicago—exclusive because no one except the members has ever heard of them: the Sittin', Starin', and Rockin' Club started by "Uncle" Tom Saxe, founder of White Castle Hamburgers, and the Noname Club, which is how we get to the story about the bird.

Here Owl, Here Owl

Mom and George had been to a party in the city with members of the Noname Club. They got home to Smith Street about 3:00 a.m., and at 5:00 a.m., her regular time to start work, Anna ran excitedly into their bedroom and woke them up. "Mrs. Heppe!" she cried. "Why you have bird in basement?!"

Mom and George looked at each other, then George got up and went down into the basement. There on the clothesline sat a snow-white owl.

George went back up the stairs and put on his boots, gloves, and hat. He then went back into the basement with Anna behind him and got a broom. Speaking softly, he said, "Here owl, here owl," at which point he put the broom handle under the owl's feet. The owl got on the handle, and George let it out the basement door.

He then went back to bed. No one ever knew how the owl got into the basement. Mom suspected one of the girls' boyfriends.

When we were kids, we dreaded going down into the basement of the house on Smith Street. It was dark and creepy. It had several rooms, including a coal room and a wine cellar. The washer and dryer were down there along with an enormous soft-water tank, which was about six feet deep and just as big around. You needed to climb a ladder to put the salt in the tank. That job was reserved for "Be a Silly," except for the day Mom thought the water was too hard. Anna and "Be a Silly" were on vacation, and Mom thought she would do it herself. She hoisted the heavy bag of salt under her arm and climbed the ladder. As she poured the salt into the tank, she lost her balance and fell head first into the tank along with the bag of salt. Luckily she didn't drown.

This One's for George

After Palatine, we moved just outside Cary, Illinois, to a place called Trout Valley. It was the former estate of John D. Hertz, founder of the Yellow Cab Company of Chicago. The estate was in the Fox River Valley and had been subdivided into beautiful home sites amid trout ponds and riding trails. It was a fun and friendly place to live and had a lot of characters. Many of our neighbors were executives and pilots with various airlines, because they knew Trout Valley wasn't under the flight path to O'Hare airport. Neighbors and friends included Chicago big-band leader Frank Masters and his wife, Phyllis, along with Richard Trentlage, who wrote the "Oscar Mayer Wiener Song."

Everyone remembers George well because when we moved in, several neighbors saw him mowing the grass while wearing a three-piece suit. Another thing they remember is one Fourth of July George fell out of the tree in the front yard. He was sawing the branch he was sitting on. Upon hearing him yell, Mom found him lying on the ground, holding his side. She ran to the neighbors' house to get help, and luckily Andre Job was home. They put George in the car and headed to the emergency room at Sherman Hospital in Elgin. While going through Algonquin, they somehow found themselves driving between the bands and floats in the Fourth of July parade, with people waving at them assuming they were participants.

Sadly, George died while we lived in Trout Valley. I was a sophomore in college. He got in the car one morning to go to work. Mom heard the car racing in the garage, and that was that. He'd had a massive heart attack, as had his father many years earlier at about the same age.

When the rescue squad arrived, Nick Warren, a dentist and neighbor, stopped to see what was going on. He reassured Mom that George was in fact dead, and would she please excuse him, as he had ice cream in the car and had to get home to get it in the icebox.

Another neighbor, Ricky Phelps, never heard the ambulance because she had been vacuuming. When Mom called to tell her George was dead, Ricky said, "Are you sure?"

When she got to the house, Ricky asked her if she would like a light scotch. Mom said, "I don't think so. It's eight in the morning." They then proceeded to try to put on Mom's eyelashes, but both sets of hands were shaking so much, they abandoned that.

Word spread quickly through Trout Valley, and by evening there were twenty-five cars on the road outside the house. Big Jim Liautaud, chairman of the Capsonic Group and father of Jimmy John of fast-food fame, was our neighbor and a great friend of Mom and George.

Jim stopped his car on his way home, walked into the house, and said, "Hey, Nance! What's the idea of having a party and not inviting me?"

Mom said, "Oh dear, honey, sit down here for a minute. I have to tell you something." After he learned what had happened, an ashen-faced Jim went home and came back with several cases of booze.

Jim Liautaud and Jack Phelps had been the two prime suspects in a caper involving George's prize tomato plant, which had grown to the size of a pumpkin. Someone put a jockstrap on it.

Marian Smith Miller

Marian Smith Miller was Mom's best friend. Marian had moved from Inverness back to Iowa, where she had grown up, after divorcing her husband, Ted. Marian and her siblings were heirs to the Iowa Electric Light and Power Company, founded by their grandfather, Isaac Smith. He also invented how to charge for kilowatt hours.

When George died, Marian flew back and stayed with us in Trout Valley. The house was so full, I had to sleep on the couch in the living room. As I was waking up the morning after George died, I heard someone in the bar, and then heard the tinkling of a drink being poured. I heard Marian say, "This one's for me." Then I heard another drink being poured, and I heard her say, "This one's for George."

After George died, Mom and Marian would travel together. Their adventures delighted my sisters and me. They would get in Marian's big Lincoln Mark VI and travel the country. One trip took them out west, where Marian had a ranch. They stayed at the Brown Palace Hotel in

Mom and Marian: "Deal me in."

Denver. The Young Republicans had just finished up a convention at the hotel, and Marian told Mom she heard the young people put pornographic magazines under the mattresses. She lifted up the mattress and voila! When the two of them finished looking at the magazine, Marian put it in her suitcase.

After they left Denver, on the way to Marian's ranch in Montana, they were forced off the road down into the median strip on the interstate. Avid gin rummy players, Marian looked at Mom and said, "Deal me in." They played a game while they waited for the state police to arrive. Marian was grateful they didn't get killed, as she didn't know what people would have thought when they found the magazine while going through her luggage.

While making their way to the ranch, they lost their way and were relieved when a line of cars appeared, which they assumed would take them to a highway. However, the line of cars happened to be a funeral procession and led them into a cemetery. After that a UPS truck came along and saved the day.

On that same trip as they were driving along, Mom said, "I keep seeing signs that say RV. What does RV mean?" Marian answered, "River view, stupid."

Marian died just a few years before Mom. Her ashes were interred in Oak Hill Cemetery in Cedar Rapids. At her request, the inscription on the box containing her ashes reads, "This doesn't suit me."

Shortly before Mom died, she said she could hear Marian's voice asking, "What's taking you so long?"

I Love You the Most

Mom's children were her number one priority, and she navigated us through the emotionally dangerous waters of adolescence, usually by making us laugh.

I think my first memories of Mom are playing hide-and-seek before I got in bed for the night. I would always hide in my closet or under the bed, and she would somehow always find me, tuck me in, and listen to my prayers:

Now I lay me down to sleep, I pray the Lord my soul to keep. If I should die before I wake, I pray the Lord my soul to take. God bless Mom, George, Kim, Sally, Pixie [dog], Toby [parakeet], Daddy, Dorane, Parkie, Dottie, Cindy [dog], Dixie [dog], Dorothy, Frank, Grandma, Boodie, and everyone in the whole world. Amen.

She would then make her way to my sisters' rooms, making sure to leave my door open so I could see the bathroom light because I was scared of the dark. I would always see her kneel and make the sign of the cross at the top of the stairs before she went downstairs for the night.

Because of my career, people often ask me if my parents were religious. I say, "Well, my mother took us to church, and my dad said 'Jesus H. Christ!' all the time." I still am not sure what the *H.* stands for.

That pretty much sums it up.

I never heard Mom say much about God. Hers was a private faith that sustained her through some very difficult years of marriage, particularly the years with my dad. She once said, "All I really wanted was to raise you kids and have a pretty house in the country. I guess I had some lessons to learn." She became a very successful Realtor when few women were in the business, and finally got that house in the country with George Heppe.

After she died, I found a well-worn prayer book filled with pictures next to her bed. I now keep it on my bedside table.

I know when I write about her, she would not want me to be overly sentimental. I can hear her saying "Let's not overdo this, now." So I won't.

Throughout childhood, we would play a game. One of us would say, "I love you the most!" The other would reply, "No, I love *you* the most!"

This time I win.

THE McKENNAS

Some of my best childhood friends from the years in Cary are the McKennas. My friend Mike's dad, Joe McKenna, was our doctor. In fact, he was just about everyone's doctor in our little community of Cary and Fox River Grove. After suffering a heart attack, he gave up his practice and became the head of the emergency room at Sherman Hospital in Elgin, the hospital in which I was born.

The McKennas were a good Catholic family and had a bunch of kids. When we were in high school, we were in choir practice and Mike told me his mother was pregnant with her ninth child, Peter. We couldn't stop laughing.

When Peter was about three, we had the brilliant idea of seeing if we could spin a top on his head. So we did. The only problem was his hair got tangled in the spinning top, pulling some hair out leaving a bald spot where his hair should have been. Just at that moment his mother, Grete, called him. We quickly put Peter's hair over the bald spot and sent him to his mother. What we didn't know is that she was going to comb his hair before they left for church. She suddenly called out, "Michael! Will!" and we quickly made our escape out the back door.

The McKennas had some entertaining neighbors. One of our favorites was Irma, who had a poodle named Coco. Coco was so fat that Irma would "walk" her by putting her in a little red wagon labeled "Coco's Taxi" and pulling her around the neighborhood.

Our parents made us get jobs for spending money and to keep us out of trouble. I had a job at Hartley's Haberdashery in downtown Cary. It was owned by our neighbor Tom Hartley, a retired airline pilot. Mike got a job at Santa's Village in nearby Carpentersville. He led the donkey for the donkey rides. His first day on the job, a little African-American boy called out to his mother, " Hey, Mom, look! It's a honky with a donkey!"

Mike's girlfriend, Susan, lived in a very large home in Inverness. Her father was a senior executive with Motorola. One night while home alone, Susan heard a noise and hit the burglar alarm. When the police arrived, they told her to stand back as they searched the house. When they got to her room, a policeman said, "This room has been ransacked." Susan said, "No, it always looks like this." There ended up being no burglar.

Mike and Susan married while Mike was in med school and I was in seminary. One night Mike and I were driving home on Route 59 between Barrington and Fox River Grove when we spotted lights in the swamp on the side of the road. We stopped the car and saw that a car had overturned and the lights were still on. Thinking the worst, Mike and I waded into the water and fortunately found the car empty. The people in it had escaped, and after we got back into our car, we came upon them walking down the road.

When we got home, we told Susan what had happened. Instead of being praised as Good Samaritans, Susan just scolded Mike for not taking off his brand-new shoes before he waded into the water. While in med school, money was tight.

As the years went by, however, fortunes changed. Well, at least theirs did. Mike became a gastroenterologist. Several years later, Mom was having a Christmas party and Susan walked in wearing a full-length mink coat and sporting a beautiful diamond bracelet. When I admired her bracelet, she said, "That's a lot of a**holes, Will."

BROADWAY BOUND

To tell you the truth, nothing much about grade school or high school interested me except my friends and music. Regarded as a talented singer, I had leads in almost every musical production. The first was *H.M.S. Pinafore*, and as a tenor I had to sing so high, my brother-in-law asked if my "jockstrap was on too tight." Then came the role as the "Soda Jerk" in *Wonderful Town*, Mr. Snow in *Carousel*, and Cornelius Hackl in *Hello, Dolly!* At Cary-Grove High School, musicals were a huge deal. So huge, in fact, that the school hired professionals from Broadway to instruct us. For a long time, I thought that musical theater would be my future.

While in high school, I toured Europe as a soloist with the Young Americans in Concert. Being gifted musically I'm sure is what got me into college because my grades were average. Mostly, though, I loved being with my friends. I really didn't care very much about where I went to college.

As I recall, I made a general application to several midwestern schools and chose Coe College in Cedar Rapids, Iowa, because my sister Sally lived there, as did my mom's friend Marian. Coe is a fine liberal arts college with a superb choral and classical music department. In my second year, I pledged the fraternity Lambda Chi Alpha and made a lot of great friends, but I never went through initiation, as I had closer "independent" friends in the dorm.

I was in the choir and continued with voice lessons, but as for the rest of my studies, I did just enough work to get by. Again, I really was more interested in having fun than studying.

My friends and I were regulars drinking Moscow Mules at the Maid Rite, a block from campus. One morning a friend and I thought we'd have a couple of "mules" before an exam. I aced it! Unfortunately, it didn't work the next time.

I also had a couple of close calls with the campus police. Like the time my roommate and I stole the college president's parking sign because we thought it would be fun to have in our room. We got caught when a security guard spotted it hanging on our wall from where he was standing outside on the quad. We didn't get in much trouble because my roommate's grandfather had once been president of Coe.

One night I drove my sister's Karmann Ghia across the center of campus as a shortcut, narrowly missing a security guard, who got the license number. When the campus police called Sally, who was sound asleep, she had no idea I had borrowed her car, which by that time was back in her garage.

I continued in the choral arts program at Coe, and it was while in the music building one day that I read about auditions being held in Davenport, Iowa. They needed a singer.

Miss Iowa Pageant

Judy Woodruff, journalist and host of the *PBS NewsHour*, has been a friend for many years. She and her husband, Al Hunt, and their children attended St. Columba's Church in Washington, DC, when I worked there. Many folks don't know Judy was crowned Young Miss Augusta 1963. We just recently laughed together that I too know the pageant world, as I was the singing host of the Miss Iowa Pageant from 1972 to 1974.

As I recall, for my opening number I wore a baby blue polyester tuxedo jacket with a ruffled tuxedo shirt, white patent leather shoes, and matching belt. One year, because of my success, I was asked to host the Miss Barrington pageant, and I got to wear a *pink* tuxedo jacket.

Betty Anderson was the talented pianist who rehearsed with me before I sang with the Wibby Fisher Orchestra on the stage at the St. Ambrose auditorium in Davenport, Iowa. Betty was great because she would vamp and cover for me, as I had a little trouble getting my cues for some of my numbers. The thing I remember best about Wibby was that he was bald, but for the performances he would paint the top of his head with black shoe polish, complete with a widow's peak and sideburns. It would bead up as he perspired during performances.

One number I remember particularly well was the one where I got on a swing and was raised high into the lights above the stage and then lowered, swinging above a couple as they tap-danced to "Tea for Two" right underneath me.

Another highlight was singing "I've Grown Accustomed to Her Face" during the bathing suit competition. And, of course, I can still remember the words to "Will She Be Miss America?"

My family was very proud of me. They came to all the pageants. One of their favorite stories to tell was about the time they were staying at the hotel with all the contestants' parents. George Heppe was swimming in the pool and one of the men swimming with him asked, "Is your daughter in the pageant?" George replied, "No, my son is." Saying nothing more, he just swam away.

University of Washington

During college a series of things happened that changed the direction my life would take.

As much as I loved my friends at Coe, the school did not have a strong musical theater component, so I searched for one that did. I settled on the University of Washington because of its fine reputation and because I loved Seattle and the Pacific Northwest, having spent every summer there since Mom and Dad's divorce. I also loved to sail and snow-ski, both of which are in close proximity to the campus. I also thought it would help me get closer to Dad.

While there I had leading roles in musical productions. Rehearsing for a role as Mr. Bigley in *How to Succeed in Business Without Really Trying*, I actually had to learn how to knit and tap-dance.

I also got a job waiting tables and singing with the Front Street Jazz Band at Doc Maynard's in historic Pioneer Square in downtown Seattle.

Lambda Chi

I again joined Lambda Chi Alpha fraternity. The Greek system offered a great way to make friends at a huge school. The Lambda Chi house is just off the main campus. Our rooms were very small, so we all slept on sleeping porches.

Right after several of us freaked out after seeing the movie *The Exorcist*, we made sure to scare one of the brothers by shaking his bed up and down in the middle of the night.

On my twenty-first birthday my roommate, Dave Fitch, arranged to have me blindfolded, kidnapped, and taken to a bar by Randy and Robin Earls, both of whom played for the University of Washington Huskies.

For a time we had a golf tee on the roof so we could hit golf balls at the Phi Delta Theta house a couple of blocks away, until it suddenly dawned on us we could kill somebody.

One year for need of a Christmas tree, we cut down an evergreen in front of the sorority house across the street. I believe we were taken to the Panhellenic Council for that. Luckily my friend Connie was the president. We had to replace the tree.

The Evidence Is Found in My Smile

I still have a chip in my front tooth from drinking wine out of a bottle at Golden Gardens Beach on Puget Sound with Dave, Darci Swanson, and Julie Topp.

Julie's parents had one of the most beautiful homes in Seattle. It was a Georgian mansion overlooking Lake Washington and Mount Rainier. It was perfect for parties, particularly when her parents were out of town. There was a swimming pool surrounded by gas torches, and when we lit them, we were lucky we didn't get blown up. One night the party got so huge that Julie's brother-in-law, who had been sleeping, came racing down the spiral staircase furious with us for letting the party get out of hand. The only thing was we couldn't take him seriously because in his fury he had thrown on Julie's mother's pink silk bathrobe with pink organza collar and cuffs.

DINE AND DASH

Fraternity parties always went into the wee hours of the morning. The two favorite places to get something to eat following a "function" were Beth's Cafe and Tai Tung. One stunt some brothers would pull was to dine and dash without paying the bill. One night at Tai Tung several of my brothers did just that—the only problem was the waiter knew I knew them and I got stuck with their bill.

MARTA

While in the fraternity, we had a cook we all loved named Marta. She was from Latvia and loved all of "her boys." All of us had nicknames that ended in *o*—e.g., Willo, Leo, Wayno, Bobo, and Marko. We all took turns helping Marta in the kitchen. Cooking and cleaning up after forty young men every day was no small task! I recall one day seeing her stirring a pot with her whole arm deep in the soup up to her shoulder. I have to confess, that did give me pause about eating the soup. She would give any gifts we would give her to her sister, who lived on Lopez Island in Puget Sound.

In the days before you could record your favorite programs, many of us would actually schedule our classes around the soap opera *All My Children*. I remember we all hated the character Phoebe Tyler. Half-eaten sandwiches would often be thrown at the television when Phoebe appeared.

A CHANGE IN DIRECTION

It was while at "U-dub," as we called it, that my academic interests were finally awakened in lectures on the History of Christianity, taught by Donald Treadgold, the chair of the Religion Department. My interest in expository writing was being influenced by my English professors, William F. Irmschir and Dorothy Bowie. The works of the poet Theodore Roethke have been a huge influence in my life. Interestingly enough, my favorite, "My Papa's Waltz," is about a child with an alcoholic father.

I regularly attended services at the Church of the Epiphany in Madrona Park and the Sunday evening choral services at St. Mark's Cathedral. The Reverend Jack Gorsuch was the rector of Epiphany and his assistant was the Reverend Laura Frazier, both of whom were wonderful preachers. Laura was one of the first women to be ordained in the Episcopal Church. Jack's nephew Neil is now a Supreme Court justice.

After I graduated, I came back home to Illinois and continued in musical productions. I had the part of Edward Rutledge in *1776* in a local summer stock theater production and then got the part of the bursar in a Michigan summer stock production of *Anything Goes* starring Dorothy Lamour, but I got homesick for my friends who were all back from college and came home to Trout Valley.

I worked at Hartley's Haberdashery in downtown Cary, Illinois, and volunteered at the Cathedral Shelter of Chicago, driving a van that picked up donations for its opportunity shop.

I decided I wanted to go to graduate school in the study of Christianity. By that time, I had been going to church on a regular basis, and went to see the rector of our church in Barrington Hills, the Reverend John Peterson. I think it was he who planted the seed of going to seminary. He recommended it might be a good idea to go, as I was trying to determine if I really believed "all this stuff." But he also saw something in me that I had yet to see in myself.

The search for meaning in my life was leading me away from a musical career.

John sent me to see the Right Reverend James Winchester Montgomery, the Episcopal Bishop of Chicago, who approved a plan. That is when I began to give up my dreams of Broadway and ended up at Virginia Theological Seminary to get a master's degree in theological studies. Those studies and what I was to discover about myself while in seminary led to my becoming an Episcopal priest.

What a Waste

As much as no one was surprised I was going to seminary, it wasn't always met with approval. I spent the summer between college and seminary living and working in Door County, Wisconsin, with my great friends

Gus and Ruth Johnson, the parents of my other best friend, Jeff. Jeff had a job driving a truck for Burns Brothers' Lumber Yard in Sister Bay. The Johnsons had a spectacular house at the tip of Door Peninsula overlooking Washington Island at Death's Door, so named because of the number of shipwrecks that have occurred there.

Seeking some sort of employment, I lasted one day stocking shelves at Crist's grocery store, for which I had to shave my head. I don't actually remember why I left. Gus then took pity on me and hired me to install insulation in their attic. After I finished the first day, he kindly explained to me that I had installed it upside down. He found other odd jobs for me to do, and when I wasn't working, he and Ruth tried to teach me how to play bridge.

Jeff and I spent many hours sailing, swimming, and drinking quarter beers and bowling at the Sister Bay Bowl. One evening while there we ran into Pat, a neighbor from Trout Valley who had recently moved permanently to Door County. She inquired as to what we were going to do with our lives. Jeff told her he was going to work as an engineer for Kimberly-Clark. That met with her approval. When I told her I was going to seminary, she said, "What a waste."

Seminary

THE PROTESTANT VIRGINIA THEOLOGICAL SEMINARY (VTS) WAS founded in 1823 by Bishop William Meade and Francis Scott Key. It sits high atop a hill on the corner of Seminary Road and Quaker Lane in Alexandria, Virginia. At its center is Aspinwall Hall, which was used as a hospital for Federal troops during the Civil War. Surrounding that are

The Rev. Jay Risk seeing Tom Atamian and me off to seminary

a refectory, dorms, a library, a chapel, and faculty housing. It is known as "the Holy Hill" by its inhabitants.

After visiting several seminaries, I chose VTS simply because I found the faculty most entertaining. There were many memorable moments from faculty, but one I remember in particular is Professor Murray Newman showing us the stone with which David killed Goliath. He had recently discovered it lying on the ground while on a walk outside of Jerusalem. It still had blood on it.

LET US PRAY

A fellow classmate was the first person I met at VTS. We were both first-years, and I was going to pick up some things at the drugstore. He needed some things too, so he asked if he could ride along. I said sure.

When we got into the car, he said, "Let us pray. Dear Jesus, we just pray you'll get us safely to the drugstore. Amen."

The drugstore was two blocks away.

When we got there, before I could open the door, he said, "Let us pray. Dear Jesus, we just want to thank you for bringing us safely here and please help us to find the things we need. Amen."

We did our shopping, and when we got back in the car, he said, "Let us pray. Dear Jesus, we just want to thank you for helping us to get the things we need [I think I was getting toothpaste], and please help us to get back safely to the seminary. Amen."

When we got back to the seminary, he said, "Let us pray. Dear Jesus, we just want to thank you for bringing us back safely. Amen."

After that I thought to myself, "Dear Jesus, I've really come to the wrong place."

"JESUS LOVES ME, THIS I KNOW"

My first year in seminary, while in a New Testament lecture with the world-renowned biblical scholar Reginald Fuller, I was sitting in the back row with George Washington Albritton Jr.—"Bubba" to his friends. Dr. Fuller was analyzing Jesus's relationship with Mary, who I assumed was his mother. Then I heard him refer to Mary Magdalene. I whispered to

Bubba, "Wait! You mean there were *two* Marys?" Bubba whispered back, "Will, don't *ever* admit you asked that to *anyone!*"

Not fancying myself any kind of biblical scholar, I take great comfort in what the theologian Karl Barth said in a lecture before he retired. When asked what the most important thing he ever learned was, he said, "Jesus loves me, this I know, for the Bible tells me so."

The other eye-opener regarding the importance about literary historical criticism occurred during the middle of a service in the seminary chapel. A lector concluded the reading with the words "the word of the Lord" when somebody called out, "Probably not!"

PREACHING CLASS

We had a class where we would write sermons and deliver them to be critiqued by our professor and classmates. In the middle of one of those sessions, one seminarian got so angry at what his classmate said about his sermon that he jumped up and chased him around the table. The other young man jumped out the window of Key Chapel to get away from him!

RANT AND CHANT

There was a class in which we would practice reciting the various liturgics in the Episcopal Book of Common Prayer. During one of them, my classmate Patricia Thomas told me a story: At the time when the minister breaks the bread in front of the congregation, instead of saying, "Christ our Passover is sacrificed for us," the minister said, "Christ our *sackover* is *pacified* for us."

Since then I rarely take my eyes off the book.

We also had a class where we sang every hymn in the hymnal. We called it "Rant and Chant." In that class we also learned who should be singing the liturgy and who should not.

GOD'S IMPERFECT JEWEL

Charles Livermore, a great friend while in seminary, was fond of saying VTS was actually a sanitarium. We didn't know it, but our families had sent us there to be cured. Ironically, a lot of truth could be found in that statement. There were a lot of crazies, and I turned out to be one of them.

Initially seminary was very difficult for me. I had never been in an academic environment that had required so much from me with regard to research and study. My grades were average at best, and, on top of that, those of us who were candidates for Holy Orders were evaluated again and again psychologically as to our suitability for the ministry. I was having trouble concentrating and preoccupied with my poor performance in the classroom.

At one point a particularly confrontational professor accused me of "hiding behind my smile." It caused me to doubt myself even more than I already did. I consulted my academic advisor, who suggested I see a counselor. I thought my chances for Holy Orders were over until my kindly spiritual advisor, former seminary dean Jesse Trotter, said, "Will, be glad this is happening to you now, instead of when you're fifty."

I was directed to a pastoral counselor, one who while treating me for depression would also take seriously questions of faith. While in therapy, what I began to understand was that I was treating my life, relationships, and seminary just as I would a *performance*. I believed I had to be flawless. My counselor had a name for it. He called it the "Superman or sh*t syndrome." I believed if I wasn't Superman, I was a piece of sh*t. Though I wasn't playing Cornelius Hackl or Mr. Bigley anymore, I was still an actor playing many roles, performing for many people and seeking the applause of my professors, the bishop, and the standing committee of the diocese. I remember playing a role once in college when I didn't understand my character and I was *terrible*. This time I realized I didn't understand *myself*.

So I began a journey of self-discovery to play my most important role . . . *being me*. It has meant the difference between *playing* a priest and *being* a priest.

My pastoral therapist led me to ask a question. It was a critical one that lies at heart of the Christian faith because of those words in the liturgy I have heard since I was a child: "On the night Jesus died for us." Why in the world would Jesus *die for us*? Even more specifically . . . *for me*?

It was then he gave me an article to read. It was titled "God's Imperfect Jewel."

It was my "lightbulb" moment.

I can't remember what the article even said—it was all in the title. I finally got it. Why *would* Jesus die for us? It is probably the most important question in my life or anyone's life for that matter, at least anyone who professes the Christian faith.

Regardless of what doubts we may have about ourselves, there is actually something about us, about you and me, *worth dying for.*

Never did I think I'd find an answer in *imperfection.* Curiously, love often manifests itself in empathy when imperfections are revealed. We are *God's imperfect jewels.*

Jesus is reported to have said in Matthew 5:24, "Be ye perfect as your heavenly Father is perfect." We are perfect in our ability to love as God loves.

We're perfect in our imperfection. Quite an oxymoron, but with God all things are possible.

All I knew was that I didn't want anyone, particularly young people, to fall into the same trap I did as a young man. I have dedicated much of my life to reminding folks *you are loved simply for who you are.* It is in those words I have found my vocation.

I'm reminded of what Bishop Montgomery once wrote to me in a letter: "Will, it's important to *know* God, not just *know about* God."

To know God is to know you are loved.

THE SEMINARY GUN CLUB

After reading what I've written so far about the seminary, it may sound as though it was horrible. It really wasn't. Sure, the academics were demanding and I went through a depression, but I made it through, due in no small part to the shenanigans of the Seminary Gun Club.

It had nothing to do with guns, but rather everything to do with friendship . . . and bourbon. *Every night* Donald Fishburne, Bill Hague, Bubba Allbritton, Chris Seitz, George Yandell, and Billy and Jennifer Shand would gather for cocktails at the apartment of Annilee Thornhill Brown, the seminary hostess. It was a fraternity of sorts but women were allowed if Annilee liked them (she wasn't too big on women in the priesthood), and Jennifer was "just fine."

Annilee was a fabulous cook, and it was a good thing because most nights we had to eat in the refectory, which Donald coined "the

The Seminary Gun Club

Annilee Thornhill Brown, the seminary hostess

regurgitory," so Annilee's "butt cut" was always a welcome respite from "mystery meat."

Annilee grew up in Alabama. Her parents died and left her orphaned at a very young age. She was raised by loving relatives, and as a young girl learned some of the funniest expressions I've ever heard:

"That one could go bear huntin' with a switch!"

"I wouldn't know him from Adam's off ox!"

"If that don't take the rag off the bush!"

"I'm busier than a bee in a tar bucket!"

"I got on the first thing smokin'!"

"Everyone that shows their teeth ain't necessarily your friend!"

"I'm gropin' around like a blind dog in a meat house!"

"I'm as nervous as a cat in a room full of rocking chairs!"

"I feel like the butt cut of destruction!"

"It looks like the wreck of the Hesperus!"

She had a knitting group with faculty wives known by us as "The Inner Apostolic Circle of the Seminary Gun Club" and also the CIA (Christian Information Agency), which included Betty Price, Mim Whitney, and Marge Blood. That's how we found out what was really going on at the seminary.

One morning after a particularly late night partying at Annilee's with the Gun Club—which happened to be the same night we sneaked into the chapel and Billy opened up every stop on the organ, waking up our homiletics professor who lived next door—I was getting some breakfast before going off to fieldwork. I sat down next to a fellow seminarian, and when I asked him how he was, he said, "Terrible!" I asked him what was wrong, and he said, "I was awake all night because of that animal bunch at Mrs. Brown's."

Luckily for us, Annilee was a favorite of the seminary dean, Cecil Woods, and his wife, Marie, which is why we probably didn't get kicked out.

ARE YOU HAPPY HERE?

Dean Cecil Woods was as genteel and gracious a person as I have ever known. Legend has it that when he had to deliver the bad news to seminarians that they were getting kicked out, he would request an evening meeting and would begin with the words, "I understand you're unhappy here."

One afternoon Billy Shand received a call from the dean's secretary. When he greeted the Gun Club that evening before his meeting, he was as white as a sheet. We all waited expectantly at Annilee's. When he returned, we were relieved to learn the meeting had nothing to do with Billy's dismissal, but rather a question having to do with the Diocese of South Carolina. Yet another cause for celebration for the Gun Club.

THE SEMINARY TRADITION

During my time at the seminary, there was what was known as "The Seminary Tradition." At the time, chapels were generally Morning Prayer with only an occasional Eucharist, and the liturgy was rarely sung except for the canticles and hymns. There were those students who preferred we have the Eucharist more frequently and referred to Morning Prayer as *unchurch*.

In response, the Reverend Charlie Price gave a homily explaining his view that the seminary liturgy didn't need to offer all things for all people. He quoted 1 Corinthians 12, saying that the seminaries of the church offered liturgy each in its own way, contributing to the whole of the body—the idea being you learn a particular tradition and learn it well.

One morning in chapel, I was introduced to something I had never before experienced, "speaking in tongues." People speaking in languages unknown to them is understood as a gift of the Spirit. Speaking in tongues *out loud* was frowned upon during seminary chapel—it was *not* part of the Seminary Tradition. That morning I was seated next to Dean Woods when one of the seminarians was overcome. Impressed, I whispered to the dean, "Was that Aramaic?" Clearly not pleased that it had occurred, he looked at me over his glasses and whispered back, "No, it was not."

I never heard it again.

SINGING IN THE PULPIT

The first time I sang in the pulpit was in seminary. A sermon I had written in homiletics class was chosen by my teacher to be preached to the entire seminary community. The sermon was about Judas and his being conflicted. I sang Judas's soliloquy from *Jesus Christ Superstar*. Needless to say, it was a bit of a shock to a very reserved community.

LOVING THE QUESTIONS

While in seminary, Professor Marianne Micks, known as Mixy, had a course I will never forget in which she encouraged us to search the Bible for the questions it asks. Certainly Jesus asked many questions of his followers and made them wrestle with the answers for themselves. Then he would tell a story—which might leave them wondering even more.

Also by telling a story he would have them use their imagination.

I think I initially approached the Bible looking for its answers more than for its questions. Mixy wrote a book titled *Loving the Questions: An Exploration of the Nicene Creed*, which I subsequently used in my classes at St. Albans.

YOUTH GROUPS

While I was in seminary, I started running youth groups. As much as I would like to think the draw was my sparkling personality and brilliant mind, what attracted the kids in a word was, and always has been . . . *food*. Pizza is always a big draw, and every youth group meeting I ever had—whether it be at St. Francis Church in Potomac, Maryland (where I did my fieldwork); St. Columba's in Washington, DC; or St. Mark's in Barrington Hills, Illinois—had to meet on Sunday nights.

Sunday night was the perfect night because the kids had no other commitments. They also could avoid doing their homework for Monday

St. Columba's youth group, Bethany Beach trip

and their parents nagging them about it. It was a perfect excuse to say to a parent, "I'm going to church." What could they say to that?

One Sunday night at St. Columba's, we met at my house and made our own pizzas. After the kids had gone, I was cleaning up and suddenly saw my clerical collars (which I kept in a beer mug) all over the counter, stained pink. The kids had used them to spread sauce on the pizzas.

Remarkably, I had gotten myself a reputation for being very successful at working with young people. Later, I learned it was probably for the wrong reasons.

While I was at St. Mark's, the youth group grew to such an extent that we were amazed. We could have as many as thirty kids on a given night. What I didn't realize until the kids, now adults, told me years later was that they were smoking pot before the meetings. They laughed at everything. In retrospect, I knew I was funny, but not that funny.

At St. Francis the kids loved going on youth group trips. We could have as many as fifty kids. What the chaperones and I didn't realize is they were hiding beer on the trips and would drink it after we went to bed.

Truth is, the chaperones also were hiding theirs.

Seriously, though, the relationships with those children and their families have continued through the years and are some of the happiest I have.

By Any Means Necessary

Parents are always trying to negotiate with kids about going to church. Youth group is a good compromise, but perhaps the funniest story I ever heard involved my friends Polly, Flossie, and Stewart Bryan. Their mother was affectionately known as "Big Red" because she was tall, with bright red hair and a personality to match.

Her children had been out very late one Saturday night attending a party. The following morning, the phone rang. Their mother took the call and said, "Yes, I'd be delighted, Reverend! Thank you so much!" She hung up the phone and said the reverend had invited her to sing in the choir that morning. Her children were dumfounded, as they knew their mother couldn't carry a tune.

"Big Red" left home early and the children raced to get dressed to get to church on time. When they arrived at church, they found their mother sitting in the front row far from the choir. Their butler knew the trick of making the phone ring and had been in on the ruse.

St. Francis

While at St. Francis, it wasn't just the children with whom I interacted. I also became great friends with some of the adults who mentored me along the way. Two of my favorites were Jack Skillman and Bob Stevens. They were supervising the construction of the new wing, and they often invited me to lunch at the Chinese restaurant across the street, which always involved a couple martinis. When I go back to Potomac, I always pay my respects in the memorial garden where Jack's ashes are interred. He's around the corner from Charlie Simpson. My great friend Marcia Eisinger has reserved the space between the two of them because they were favorites of hers.

Pam Ramsay was the senior warden at St. Francis and as wise a person as I have ever known. One night after I had delivered one of my first homilies, Pam and I searched all over the church trying to figure out how to turn the lights off. Pam looked at me and said, "You better get used to it, Will. In the church you frequently go from the sublime to the ridiculous." No truer words were ever spoken.

The Cigar Box

Among my possessions I have an old cigar box that belonged to my stepfather, George Heppe. Since high school I have kept special things in that box. I can barely close it now. In it I have my "honor program" pin from Cary-Grove High School, the key to my hotel room from my high school trip to France, and letters from Mom, Dad, and George. There are notes from President and Mrs. George H. W. Bush. Those sorts of things. But one thing in particular gives me pause.

The day I graduated from seminary, the kids in my youth group at St. Francis surprised me by coming to the ceremony. I didn't know they ditched school to do it. Neither did their parents.

Will,

How have you been? You must be busy.
I could have sworn I told you to write
back in my last letter. I hope you got it.
I still going out with Diana D. We're still
having a great time. We just had our 3 month
anniversary on February 10th ___ was the last day
of the ski ___ both went on it
and had a ___ didn't get me a
valentines da ___ me something alot
better. I ga ___ it a "love letter,"
thats what s ___ lly got my license
last week (2) ___ a chance to drive
by myself over ___ picked her up
at her house, ___ e she wasn't
there. I had t ___ 15 min. before
she came home ___ was out shopping for shoes
with some lady down the street. After she got
home, we left almost immediately. We drove to
my house and waited around until my parents went
out, then Michele's honey (Walt) came over and
the four of us went out to Armands (a pizza place).
I don't know if you know what Armands is. Diana
and I were going to go to a movie, but... we
decided we could have more fun at home, (my house

over

The picture and letter from Chris Mion

Among them was Christopher Mion, the youngest child of John and Nancy Mion, of Potomac, Maryland. Chris, a student at Walt Whitman High School (when he went), was full of fun and adored by his five older siblings. His favorite store was Al's Magic Shop in Washington, DC, and he would entertain us regularly by performing tricks. He got in trouble once at school for blowing sneezing powder in a teacher's face. But the thing I remember most about Chris is that he was in love, and I have the letter to prove it. It's in the box.

Her name was Diana. Her mother, Barbara, was a fellow student at the seminary. After I graduated and moved back to Illinois, Chris wrote me a long letter professing his love for Diana. I kept the letter because I thought one day it would be a riot to read it back to him. I never got the chance.

Chris was killed in a car accident while heading back home to Potomac from DC. The young man who was driving the car lost control at the corner of River Road and Wilson Lane.

What the letter means to me now is manyfold. It speaks of the sweetness of young love to be sure, but it also speaks of the preciousness of life.

Many years later, while I was at St. Albans, we would have retreats for the seniors. I would have them bring "their life in a box." They too had letters, pictures, whatever they could fit, even game balls and lucky socks. They all heard about Chris.

His parents, John and Nancy, remain very close friends of mine and I marvel at their deep faith. What they have taught me is to not be afraid to continue to laugh when we speak of people we love who have died. For in so doing, we experience again the joy they brought into our lives.

Nancy recently said something that, when I think about it, is as profound a statement of faith as I have ever heard, from someone who has known the unimaginable grief of having three children die: "I had six, I never thought I'd have to give back three."

ANGELS

One day, while browsing through the seminary bookstore, I came across a book that literally had my name on it. It was not in the stack of books required in the curriculum and I hadn't ordered it. The book was *Wishful*

Thinking: A Theological ABC by Frederick Buechner. I picked it up and began to read. It immediately captivated me. Since that time I quote it often, frequently give it as a gift, and have used it in my classes.

Could it have been an angel that put my name on that book? It fits Buechner's definition. He claims we don't see angels because we don't expect to. All I know is I keep it on my bookshelf, right next to my Bible and my Book of Common Prayer.

Leaving Seminary

When you graduate from the seminary, you are thrust back into the real world. Back in the parish, nobody much cares who Tertullian was or what was argued at the Council of Nicaea.

My great friend Suzanne Robinson once told me a story about a young priest just out of seminary who worked really hard on a sermon on the Doctrine of the Atonement. As he was greeting the congregation after the service, an elderly woman came up to him and said, "That was a really nice sermon, Father, but what I really want to know is, how is Jesus going to change my life?"

If I had been that young priest, I would have then told her how Jesus changed my life, along with the parishioners at my first parish, St. Mark's Episcopal Church in Barrington Hills, Illinois.

It Gives Us All Hope!

When you're done with seminary, one of the steps to ordination involves taking the General Ordination Examination (GOE) of the Episcopal Church. It is meant to see if you have mastered several areas of theology.

I failed every area.

I guess I shouldn't have been surprised. I have never tested well. I thought I was done for. That was until three of my professors in particular jumped to my aid: the Reverend Dr. Charles P. Price, the Reverend Dr. Reginald Fuller, and the Reverend Dr. David Scott. Luckily for me, all powers of ordination lie in the hands of the bishop, and whatever arguments they made in my defense must have worked. I had some oral examinations and did fine. I am eternally grateful to them and, of course, the bishop.

Ironically, I ended up a teacher and chaplain myself. Years later when I was back at the seminary for convocation, I was introduced to a seminarian who said to me, "You're Will Billow! You're famous!"

"For what?" I asked.

"For failing all your GOEs," he replied. "It gives us all hope."

St. Mark's Barrington Hills

ORDINATION

AFTER SEMINARY, FINAL APPROVAL FOR ORDINATION COMES FROM THE Standing Committee, a governing body within each diocese, and the bishop. It generally occurs some months after you start your first job. There are actually two ordinations: one to the diaconate and the next to the priesthood.

Ordination actually occurs with what is called the "laying on of hands," which is based on the scriptural account of how the apostles received the Holy Spirit from Jesus. When ordained as a deacon, the bishop lays his hands on your head and says a prayer. When ordained as a priest, the hands of all bishops and clergy present do the same. You are meant to feel the weight of the job.

Before our ordinations, all of us candidates in the Diocese of Chicago were required to go on a silent retreat. That is where I met two of my great friends, the Reverend Johnson and the Reverend Holland. We weren't much for the silent part. After our meals and meditations, we sneaked out to a local bar. Luckily we didn't get caught by the retreat leaders, which might have caused some disciplinary action. After all, Jesus did say, "Be wise as a serpent and innocent as a dove," which has come in handy from time to time throughout my ministry.

My ordinations were grand and glorious affairs held at the Episcopal Cathedral in Chicago with many of my friends and parishioners attending, all of whom lined up to receive a blessing from me after the service. It was then I realized they sought something *through* me. That something is the Holy Spirit. It is extremely humbling. It is a priest's greatest responsibility.

MINK AND MANURE

I was walking through the darkness of this life with a little candle of faith to light my way . . . and then a theologian came . . . and blew it out.

—ANONYMOUS

That quote was on a card someone gave me at my ordination to the priesthood. It is a favorite of mine and an important reminder to clergy to not lose touch with their parishioners. My first job out of seminary was at St. Mark's Episcopal Church in Barrington Hills, Illinois, and luckily the congregation kept my feet planted firmly on the ground.

Barrington Hills is an affluent community consisting of rolling and wooded estates, each on a minimum of five acres, fifty miles northwest of Chicago. It is home to many of Chicago's most prominent families, who move there because of its beauty and its privacy. It is also home to the Riding Club of Barrington Hills, the Fox River Valley Hunt, and the Barrington Hills Country Club.

St. Mark's, in the heart of Barrington Hills, was founded by some disgruntled parishioners of St. Michael's, the Episcopal church in the town of Barrington, because they didn't like the "high church" liturgy. So they purchased some land on Ridge Road and had their services in the Goldmans' barn across the road while the church was being constructed. Hence St. Mark's was known in the Episcopal Diocese of Chicago as "the mink and manure parish."

St. Mark's rector, John Peterson, was the clergyperson who had walked me through Holy Orders (the process of becoming a priest) and had sponsored me for ordination. Mom began attending St. Mark's after George's death, and I attended with her while home from college. John hired me upon my graduation from seminary, and within a year he took a new job in Florida, leaving me as priest-in-charge while they began a search for a new rector.

I had an absolute ball working there. Many parishioners were family friends. They were kind, understanding, and funny. It was a healthy and happy place and taught me what a parish could really be if you did it right. John did.

He made me make cold calls on each parishioner, even though he confessed he once called on a woman and when he arrived at the kitchen door, she was scrubbing the floor in her girdle. After hearing that, I always rang the front doorbell.

During my very first sermon at St. Mark's, Ned fell asleep and snored louder than I spoke. His wife, Marjorie, later apologized and said, "Ned has narcolepsy." I never found out if that was really true. And if I needed another reminder on brevity, I had within eyeshot Bill, president of a prominent railroad company, sitting in the choir and waving his finger round in the air to tell me to "wrap it up!" He had a regular Sunday morning foursome and a tee time to get to at the club.

I attribute my religious sensibilities to Mom. She eschewed gossip and church politics, and when I became vicar of St. Mark's, she would leave before coffee hour.

After my first sermon, I asked her what she thought. She said, "Honey, we understood it the first time you said it. Just say what you have to say, then sit down and be quiet."

Since then my sermons are rarely more than five to seven minutes. And you know what? People never complain. I think that prepared me well for preaching to adolescent boys for twenty-five years. And are boys interested in church politics? Not one bit.

DOING DONUTS

Kay Klicker and Liz Stark were the parish secretaries. They were best friends. Kay was from Minnesota, very prim and Lutheran, someone you might imagine lived in Garrison Keillor's Lake Wobegon.

Liz was just the opposite. Before she moved to Barrington, she had a radio talk show in Greenwich, Connecticut. She loved her scotch. She was hard of hearing and as a result was loud. She could play piano by ear, which she did regularly during the work day in the parish hall next to our offices. We would frequently sing show tunes together.

One day on our way out to lunch, I was explaining that the kids in the youth group had been "doing donuts" in the gravel parking lot on Sunday night. Kay had never heard of such a thing. Liz and I looked at each other, grabbed Janice Lee, the assistant rector, and said "Let's go!" I was driving. Yelling "Whee!" went spinning several times around the church parking lot. I don't think Kay ever got over it.

CLUELESS

The Reverend Janice Lee was an assistant along with me at St. Mark's. She was one of the first women ordained in the Diocese of Chicago. She had lived for many years in Barrington Hills with her husband, Bland, and their daughter, Torie, and was a longtime member of St. Mark's when she sought ordination. At the time, some parishioners were skeptical of the idea of female priests—that is until they met Jan. They loved her.

Being newly ordained as I was, Jan and I were clueless about how to run a parish when John Peterson announced he was leaving to go to another church. We were fortunate to have the wise counsel of Heath Davis, the senior warden. Luckily he had a great sense of humor after the stunt we pulled.

As you enter St. Mark's, you are struck by the beautiful Palladian window behind the altar. It has not always been visible, having been concealed by a red velvet curtain for many years. I'm not sure when it occurred to me that there even was a window there, but Jan and I, not realizing there was a building and grounds committee or that certain things require vestry approval, got the idea to take down the curtain. So one day we just did it.

Unbelievably *nobody* complained. Everyone loved it! But Heath gently explained to us that we might have acted impetuously.

TAKING UP THE COLLECTION

Georgia Weidenmiller and her sister Jean Buhlman took up the collection every Sunday morning at the eight o'clock service. Jean, a former dancer, would always do a little tap and a dip when presenting the plates. Then, in the most sacred part of the service, the two of them would proceed to pour the contents of the collection plates out in the back pew (coins and all) and count the money *out loud*—"Fifteen, sixteen, seventeen . . . No! Eighteen! Oops! Oh hell, start over! Ha ha!"—and start the counting all over again.

The Blessing of the Hounds
St. Mark's was also the place where I first performed "The Blessing of the Hounds." It is a long-standing English tradition to bless the hounds at the beginning of fox-hunting season. I went out to the Benninghovens' estate, where they had me stand on a crate to do it so the dogs didn't lift their legs on my vestments.

The Skateboard Sermon
To make a point during a children's sermon at St. Mark's, I brought a skateboard out from behind the pulpit, ran, and jumped on it, vestments flying. The lesson that day was St. Paul's letter encouraging "members of the body together." Never very adept on a skateboard, I'm lucky I didn't break my neck.

Diving into the Pulpit
On another Sunday morning early in my ministry, I was giving a sermon about falling in love and describing a first date. I was describing a romantic evening and *meant* to say you stay up all night but instead said "and you stay all night." Realizing what I said, I didn't correct myself—I literally dove down into the pulpit and hid from the congregation, which had erupted into gales of laughter. When I reemerged, the laughter continued for quite a while. At the time, I was dating the daughter of the senior warden.

Wearing Your Collar
One night I got a phone call in the middle of the night that a parishioner was dying and I had to drive to Sherman Hospital in Elgin. I threw on jeans and a sweatshirt, grabbed a prayer book, and got pulled over for speeding. Trying to get out of the ticket, I explained I was an Episcopal priest. The policeman said, "Yeah, and I'm the Virgin Mary." I can't remember if I got a ticket or a warning, but if at all possible, I try to have a collar ready to go.

Super Stud

One of my parishioners who became a great friend is David Judd Nutting. He is the son of Harold Nutting, who was the executive vice president of Marshall Field in Chicago. Dave has always followed his own path. During his teenage years, while the Chicago social scene might have required debutant balls and white tie and tails, he was much more comfortable avoiding all of that. He is the only person I know who, other than Elvis, had a pair of blue suede shoes. I think he had an orange jumpsuit as well.

While the expectation might have once been that he would become a corporate executive, luckily Dave's parents appreciated the eccentricities of their son and Dave became an inventor. And a very successful one at that. Early in his career he designed the first SUV, the Jeep Wagoneer, and then as consultants to Bally/Midway, his design group invented the first microprocessor video-game hardware system. The first games invented were *Gun Fight* and *Sea Wolf*, pioneers in the video-game industry.

I lived across the street from Dave on Ridge Road, where he lived with his wife, Phyllis, and their daughter, Lisa, in a beautiful yellow colonial surrounded by a fenced-in pasture. For several years there was an orange helicopter in the front pasture. Dave was designing it and intended to market it as a kit that others could build as well. The reason it was in the pasture was because it couldn't fit in the garage, which Dave discovered the first time he tried to move it to see if it would fly and they had to take off the front of the garage to get it out. One year at Thanksgiving, he was flying it and crashed into the hill on the side of the pasture. Mom, who was watching while finishing her pie, put her plate down and asked, "Is it supposed to do that?"

One year to surprise them at Christmas, I got several long extension cords and decorated the helicopter with lights. Dave retaliated by attaching a license plate cover to the back of my car that said "Super Stud." I discovered this after driving to a diocesan convention in my clergy collar and wondered why folks were pointing and laughing at me on the Northwest Tollway.

I have always admired folks with talent like Dave's. Suffice it to say, I have never had much luck with mechanical things. In high school when I worked at Hartley's Haberdashery in Cary, Illinois, the owner, Tom Hartley, wrote on a college recommendation: "I wouldn't trust Will with a power mower, but he'd do fine with a push type."

I spent a lot of time with Dave. One day I was following him around his workshop and suggested to him that I learn a trade or be his apprentice, saying something like, "After all, Jesus was a carpenter . . ."

Dave looked at me over his glasses and said, "Don't bother. I can't preach."

He has recently authored a book that posits quantum physics reveals how God thinks.

THE BLACK EYE

While at St. Mark's, a parishioner, a young woman who had recently married, called to make an appointment with me. I knew her family well. She was an exceptionally talented person who excelled in academics and athletics (baseball) while in college.

She came into my office and sat down. When she removed her sunglasses, I saw she had a huge black eye, which she had recently received not from an errant pitch, but from her husband. It wasn't the first time.

Unfortunately, when it had happened previously, the clergyperson from whom she sought advice told her, "Just try to love him more."

Obviously that turned out *not* to be the right advice, and frankly I'm not even sure what that meant.

This was out of my league, so I consulted Barrington Family Services. They were extremely helpful. The woman with whom I spoke said, "Tell her to get out *now*!"

Fortunately she did, and moved home with her parents until her divorce. The only thing I then had to worry about was her father's fury toward her ex.

Together we all learned more about physical abuse, including how statistics show that the chances of having a successful relationship in its aftermath are very poor. But she continued in counseling and is now happily remarried and the mother of two children. And she still plays baseball.

COULD I SPEAK TO YOU A MOMENT?

Shortly after I was ordained and working at St. Mark's, I was in my newly acquired clerical collar having lunch with my mom at Hackney's Restaurant on Route 12 in Lake Zurich, Illinois. A young man was sitting at the next table with his two children, a little boy and a toddler in a high chair. The man came over to our table and asked, "Reverend, could I speak to you a moment?" I said, "Sure," and excused myself to join him at his table.

When we sat down he said, "This morning my wife went down into the basement to get the laundry. The basement was flooded. When she touched the dryer, she was electrocuted and died. We are on our way to my parents. I wonder if you would say a prayer with us."

In my own shock I did offer some sort of prayer, but this is one of those heartbreaking situations in which, I've realized, even if words fail (and they often do), what matters most is just the fact that you're there. It also reveals what a clerical collar represents to those who see you in it; you have to be prepared for the unexpected. It was also a strong message to me about whom it is I represent.

MIMI

Mimi was among my family's closest friends and our neighbor on Inverway Road. She came from a very wealthy Cincinnati family. Her father had been an executive at Procter & Gamble. Her mother bought two new Cadillacs every year just in case something happened to one of them.

To say Mimi was blunt would be putting it mildly. She was the first person to tell me I had BO and I needed to use deodorant. Very smart and attractive, she had her pilot's license and flew in competitions with Marion Jayne, another neighbor in Inverness. Marion's husband, George, had been shot dead in their basement by a hitman who had been hired by his own brother, Silas. His first attempt had failed when he had a bomb planted in George's car at their stable. It instead killed a young woman who rode horses with my sister Kim. George had asked her to bring his car around.

I remember as a young child seeing Mimi in church regularly. Her son "Three" was my good friend and an acolyte along with me, and we went to confirmation class together. Mom once told me a funny story Mimi told about herself: One Sunday morning in church, having been out "very late" the night before, her younger son, "Weary," leaned over and whispered to her, "Mom . . . Your neck looks like a turkey's neck." Mimi started to cry.

Many years later, after I was ordained and working at St. Mark's in Barrington Hills, Mimi called the office and asked if she could come and see me. Her daughter Carol had recently died of cancer in her mid-thirties, leaving a young son, Colby. Mimi had just been out to Colorado for Carol's memorial.

When she came into the office, she was, as always, very matter-of-fact. She said, "Will, I just came back from Carol's service in Colorado and people said very wonderful things about her, but I wonder if you would read through the burial service with me. I just need to hear she went somewhere."

FAREWELL TO BARRINGTON

In 1981 while still at St. Mark's, the Reverend Bill Tully called me to see if I would consider coming to work with him. Bill had been associate rector at St. Francis Church in Potomac, Maryland, where I had done my fieldwork as a seminarian. He had been called to be the rector of St. Columba's Church in Washington, DC, following the tenure of Bill Swing, who had been elected Bishop of California. I knew St. Columba's by reputation and had, in fact, sung in a recital there with Gloria Waggoner, a soprano with a spectacular voice, whose husband, Jim, was my classmate at VTS.

I believe Bill Tully to be brilliant, a visionary, and I knew I could learn a lot from him. St. Columba's had a large staff and the largest Sunday attendance of any Episcopal church in Washington. Plus, it had a fantastic music program led by Judith Dodge, a well-known DC musician.

I was curious, even though it would mean leaving St. Mark's and all the folks I loved and who had taught me so much. It meant leaving home. By that time, having declined the possibility of becoming rector of St. Mark's, the church had called a new rector. He was somewhat old-fashioned, even telling Jan she should not wear open-toed shoes while giving out Communion because she "looked like a hooker." After that I decided to go for the interview.

After my interview, I was offered the job of assistant rector of St. Columba's. I said yes.

St. Columba's

St. Columba's Episcopal Church sits on the corner of Albemarle and 42nd Streets in the Tenleytown neighborhood in northwest Washington, DC. At the time I worked there, it had the largest Sunday attendance of any Episcopal church in Washington and had a congregation that included many people of note. President and Mrs. George H. W. Bush, George F. Will, David Ignatius, Judy Woodruff, Al Hunt, Colbert King, and White House chief of staff James A. Baker III and his wife, Susan, were counted among its parishioners.

Sargent House

When I interviewed to become an assistant at St. Columba's, one of the first things I did was attend lunch at something called Sargent House. It was a luncheon group that met every Wednesday, primarily consisting of old folks and the St. Columba's staff, who gathered around tables set up in the vestibule outside the main office under the painting of Anna Purna Tucker, the founder. After I got the job, I wouldn't miss it!

Katherine Early made the tuna sandwiches every week, and they would appear at noon along with the lemonade, chips, tea, and cookies. From time to time we were treated to an authentic English trifle for dessert made by Charlie Baggott, who in his younger years served English royalty as a valet. Esther Barr, Helen Petit, Craig Eder, George and Charlie Fletcher, and the Baggotts would regale us with stories of old . . . and we would laugh and laugh and listen to the history of the church they loved and how their lives were entwined with it. They told me of how attendance was so low at one point, "you could shoot a cannon off inside the church and not hit a soul" until Randy Mengers, the former rector, built a nursery school adjacent to the church and saved it.

THE FLETCHERS

One of my favorite stories came from George and Charlie Fletcher about their parents, who were founders of the parish.

One Christmas Eve many years ago, Washington, DC, was in the midst of a huge snowstorm. It was certainly not a night to be driving, and unfortunately their mother was in charge of the Christmas Eve dinner at the church. The Fletcher homestead sits atop Tenley Circle, one of the highest points in DC, just above St. Columba's. Their father bundled up his wife, the turkey, stuffing, gravy, cranberry sauce, and pie on a sled for the trip to the church. He pulled the sled a good part of the way on level ground, but when he got to the top of the hill on Wisconsin Avenue, the sled took off on its own down the hill. He chased it, but to no avail. The sled hit the side of the church, and Mrs. Fletcher ended up wearing most of what she had prepared for Christmas dinner. Their father said, "I didn't know whether to serve the turkey or Nellie!"

Every week until well into his nineties, George would gather flower arrangements thoughtfully reconfigured after church on Sunday for home delivery until one day he mistook his accelerator for the brake and took out several parking meters and a fire hydrant on Wisconsin Avenue. After that, I think he continued to deliver the flowers but someone else drove.

ESTHER'S COLD REMEDY

At Sargent House lunch one day, the air was permeated with the smell of Vicks VapoRub. Upon inquiry we discovered Esther Barr had a terrible chest cold but did not want to miss Sargent House, so she created a poultice and had slathered her chest with Vicks, carefully covering it with cellophane so as not to get any on her dress.

WITH GRATITUDE TO GEORGE F. WILL

Young clergy are known for oversharing in the pulpit, and I was as guilty as the next person. In one of my first sermons at St. Columba's, I was telling the congregation about my experience in therapy. I had been suffering from depression and told them that after several meetings with me, the therapist had said, "Will, you have the capacity to find the turd in the jar of Tootsie Rolls."

As I recall, there was an audible gasp from the congregation. When the service was over, George F. Will, a parishioner and now a longtime friend, must have known I would be in need of some support in the coming days—at least one person threatened to leave the parish. Greeting me at the door following the service, George said, "Will, I want you to know that turd is a perfectly acceptable English word."

On Monday morning when I entered my office, I found a mason jar filled with Tootsie Rolls with an unwrapped one in the middle—a gift from David Hardman, headmaster of the Potomac School, and his wife, Mary.

The Nursery School

Karen, the head of St. Columba's Nursery School, asked the clergy of the parish if we would reenact the "First Thanksgiving" for the children. We happily obliged. Craig Eder was Pilgrim Father, Louise Lusignan was Pilgrim Mother, Bill Tully was Indian Father, and Lisa Wheeler was Indian Mother. I worked behind the scenes with the necessary props for our production. Let me just say, knowing what I now know, for educated people, we reenacted every negative stereotype of which people are capable.

But, the worst thing we did was pretend to shoot the turkey, then dropped a rubber chicken from the balcony and had it fall *plop!* at the feet of the children below. After our performance, a furious Karen Strimple came storming up the stairs and strongly suggested that we all take a course in early childhood education.

As chaplain to the nursery school, I was to be present for whatever pastoral issues presented themselves to the faculty, staff, and students. One morning when we arrived, one of the teachers discovered that Cassiopeia, our floppy-eared bunny and a favorite of the children, had died in the night. With only minutes to go before carpool drop-off time, Karen and I raced around, letting teachers know. We then gently removed

"Cassie" from her cage and wrapped her in a blue-checkered tablecloth, and later that morning gathered all the children together to have a little service.

As I looked over those assembled, I asked, "Is everybody here?"

One of the children in the back answered, "Everybody's here . . . but Cassie."

"PENNIES FOR HEAVEN"
One Stewardship Sunday I got all the clergy of the parish to sing and dance with brass collection plates to the tune of "Pennies from Heaven." I rewrote the words "Pennies *for* Heaven." Bill Tully, the rector, said it was one of the most successful Stewardship Sundays ever. I have a mental picture of him dancing with a collection plate on his head along with Elisa Wheeler, Craig Eder, and Louise Lusignan.

DON'T LOOK NOW!
For the Easter Vigil, we would distribute small candles for everyone in the congregation to hold. One year Bill Tully and I were sitting next to each other, facing the congregation, when he leaned over to me and said, "Don't look now, but I think Ethel just lit her hair on fire." Sure enough, she had. Her daughter Kathy was beating the flames out with her program. Luckily Ethel was OK.

MOP AND GLOW
At the end of every service, the minister would raise his or her hand and bless the congregation by making the sign of the cross. At that moment, little Andrew Fitzgerald would say, "Mop and glow." (At the time, Mop & Glo television commercials featured someone moving their hand in a circular motion similar to a priest blessing the congregation.)

ICK!
Preparing children to receive Communion is always tricky, especially when they hear the words "body" and "blood." Some just go along with it, but others meet the whole idea with a lot of hesitation and skepticism. We would let them try the wafers ahead of time. However, one of the kids

missed the practice and while trying his first one at the altar rail, yelled out, "Ick! Mom! It tastes like cardboard!"

A Special Guest

On one particular Saturday, Mrs. Bush called Bill Tully to see who would be preaching the next day, as she was bringing a guest. The guest was the Reverend Billy Graham. As it turned out, our preacher that day was to be our seminarian, Eddie Ard, and it would be his first sermon! Bill didn't have the heart to tell Eddie about our special guest until right before the service, because he knew Eddie wouldn't have slept the night before. Eddie had grown up listening to Reverend Graham. Before he ascended into the pulpit, I recommended to Eddie that he best not drop the F-bomb.

Christmas Pageants:
The First Family Meets the Holy Family

On Christmas Eve at St. Columba's we had a tradition, as do many churches, of reenacting the scene at the manger. Joseph would lead Mary and baby Jesus on our wheeled plaster-of-paris donkey named Willy from the narthex of the church all the way up the aisle to the chancel. They were followed by all the children of the parish, dressed as animals and angels. It always went well, except for the first year of George H. W. Bush's presidency. George and Barbara Bush were parishioners, and someone neglected to tell the Secret Service about the journey of the Holy Family and Willy. All they saw were hooded figures approaching the president's pew. They reacted rather quickly, but President and Mrs. Bush assured them all was well and the procession continued.

One of my mom's favorite stories involved a little boy playing the innkeeper in his church's Christmas pageant. As Joseph and Mary approached him, Joseph would say, "Hello, my name is Joseph and this is my wife Mary. As you can see, she is great with child. Is there any room for us in the inn?" The innkeeper's response was to be, "No, I'm sorry, there is no room for you in the inn." Rehearsing this line for the umpteenth time, the little boy felt terrible about it. During the performance, when Joseph asked if there was any room in the inn, the little boy responded, "No, I'm sorry, there is no room for you in the inn, *but would you like to come in for a drink?*"

Several Christmases ago, I was the guest of my great friends Betty Ann and Corky Crovato at Casa de Campo golf resort in the Dominican Republic, along with their sons, Doug and Brad, Brad's wife Franny, and their four young boys, the youngest, Michael, a newborn. When going to church didn't seem feasible, we decided to have our own pageant. Michael was perfect for the role of baby Jesus, and we found the perfect basket for a manger. Brad and Franny played Joseph and Mary. The other three boys, Alex, Tyler, and William, wore bathrobes and played the three kings, bearing their gifts of gold (Betty Ann's jewelry box), frankincense (pronounced "circumference" by William), and myrrh. Betty Ann was the angel Gabriel, with Corky playing the innkeeper. I narrated and Doug filmed.

The staff at our villa were delighted to come to the pageant. As we made our journey around the swimming pool to Bethlehem, the exchange went something like this:

Joseph (Brad): "Is there any room at the inn?"

Innkeeper (Corky): "Will you forgive my golf debt?"

Joseph: "No."

Innkeeper: "Well then I don't have any room. Go sleep in the barn."

In a recent pageant I attended at Christ Church, Gordonsville, Virginia, the young woman playing Mary was about two feet taller than Joseph, and as they made their way down the aisle, it was clear Mary was having a bit of a struggle walking. My friend Flossie and I worried that she was physically challenged and we prayed she would make it, and she did! After the service her mother explained that her daughter had gotten her first pair of high heels for Christmas and insisted on wearing them for the first time for her performance.

CHILDREN'S SERMONS:
WITH A LITTLE HELP FROM PRESIDENT BUSH

Children's sermons are always fun. One Easter at St. Columba's, to help me take the children on a journey around the parish, Kathy Burke made an absolutely gorgeous felt banner. We went through the congregation

Easter Sunday Journey at St. Columba's

looking for brightly decorated felt eggs to place on the banner. President Bush adores children and was always a good sport when I needed a "plant" in the congregation. He tucked his egg in his handkerchief pocket, and the children were delighted when he pretended he didn't know it was there.

St. Columba's is where I tried to perfect the art of the children's sermon. To tell you the truth, they are my favorite part of any service because the minister has absolutely no control over what the children are going to say or do. It's very important to sit on the steps of the chancel at their level. No matter what theological point you're trying to make, one of the kids steals the show, such as the time Victoria Will kept twirling around and around because she had on a new Easter dress!

Sometimes the clergyperson tries too hard and the analogies are really a stretch (same is true with adult sermons). There is a great story told about a priest giving a children's sermon. He had all the young children sit with him on the steps of the chancel and said, "Kids, I have a question for you. What's brown and fuzzy, sits in a tree, and eats nuts?"

All the kids looked thoughtfully at one another, and after a moment he called on a little boy who had his hand raised. The boy said, "Well, I know the answer is Jesus, but it *sounds* like a squirrel to me."

SUNDAY SCHOOL

It's "hats off" to Sunday school teachers! One of my former students wrote of a time her teacher asked all of the children, "Who loves you the most?" They all guessed the usual, moms and dads. When the teacher said the answer was God, my student wrote that she never again trusted the words of an adult.

Another great story involves a child coming home from a Sunday school class in Chicago. His dad asked him what he learned that day, and the boy said, "Jesus is sneaking through Humboldt Park." Curious, the next Sunday the dad asked the teacher what the lesson had been. The teacher answered, "Jesus is seeking a humble heart."

And then there's the famous story of the teacher asking what God's name is. One of the children answered "Hallowitz." *Our Father who art in Heaven, Hallowitz be thy name . . .*

WITH THANKS TO BARBARA BUSH

With thanks to Barbara Bush, I'm still here—living, I mean. I don't think she ever knew she literally saved my life.

Thanks to the Bush/Walker clan, for a few summers I spent a month as interim summer rector at St. Ann's Episcopal Church in Kennebunkport. It is the church the Bush family attends when they are in residence in Maine in the summer.

The church is a lovely stone chapel, which seats about two hundred people. One of the remarkable things about it are its exquisite stained glass windows, one of which includes real seashells. The chapel sits on a point just below Walker's Point, which is home to the Bush family compound. It also has an outside chapel, which is often used for the early morning service. If you're having the service outside, the linens for Communion usually have to be weighted down because of the wind. And if you write your notes for your homily on pieces of paper, you can just forget it—they will blow away. Unfortunately I found this out the hard

Will "on the rocks" at Walker's Point. PHOTO COURTESY OF BARBARA BUSH

way, and I am not a particularly good extraneous speaker. But, I digress (which incidentally my students love, but does not bode well for folks in the pews) . . .

The rectory of the church where I lived is beautiful and is itself on a point. It is a grand home with many bedrooms and large spaces in which to entertain. The house was built for the Nesmith family of Lowell, Massachusetts, and at one time was owned by Atwater Kent, the American inventor and radio manufacturer, who was rumored to not have thought much of his neighbors in the church next door. Supposedly it was he who planted the row of trees shielding the church from the rectory. The home was acquired by the church from a later owner through a loan from the G. H. Walker Foundation.

A little farther down the ocean drive, the view of the Bushes' home at Walker's Point is quite dramatic. Across a small harbor, you can see an American flag flying high in front of the main house. The house, surrounded by several cottages where the Bush children and their families stay when they visit. Doro Bush Koch, who is a great friend of mine, spends a good part of her summer there.

You enter the property through a security gate. As you arrive at the front door, there is a lovely garden that Mrs. Bush took care of. The house offers some protection for the garden, as it can be very windy. When you enter the house, which appears very grand from the road, you are struck by how normal it is. It is lovely and warm, reflecting the personalities of its occupants. It is a happy home geared toward entertaining a large family. There is a brightly colored great room with large windows that look out over the rocks to the ocean beyond. Mrs. Bush once took a picture of me standing on the rocks with that magnificent view behind me (see previous page).

After one Sunday service, President and Mrs. Bush invited me over for brunch with several others. It was a beautiful but chilly morning on the point. When I arrived, Barbara, who was known to be direct, said to me, "Will, it's sixty-two degrees and you're perspiring." I said something like, "We're all perspirers in my family," which we are, but she thought I ought to have it checked out.

At the time, I was in relatively good shape. I had a regular jogging group in DC, which included Chan Tagliabue and John Womack. We ran regularly on the towpath just above Glen Echo at the Sycamore Store to the lock at the beginning of Georgetown. I jogged regularly in Maine on the roads surrounding Walker's Point.

When I got back to Washington, I went to see Alec Chester, my doctor, and I told him what Mrs. Bush had said. He took my wrist and felt my pulse, listened for a moment, and said, "Are you sure you feel OK?" I said, "Yes, I feel the way I always do." He said, "Come with me," and walked me directly into the office of Ramin Oskoui, who became my cardiologist.

The diagnosis was atrial fibrillation, or AFib. Just recently I had a cardiac ablation, which seems to have corrected it.

The reason I write this is because I know there are a lot of people, even those who are in good shape, who are unaware they have this problem, and it is very dangerous.

So with thanks to Barbara Bush, I'm still here, perspiring much less and very grateful.

DRIVING TO AN EARLY GRAVE

One of my favorite funeral stories involves the Bush family. It occurred during the funeral of George H. W. Bush's uncle Louis Walker, or "Uncle Lou" as he was affectionately called by the president. The burial took place in a cemetery in Maine, with the memorial service following at St. Ann's Episcopal Church in Kennebunkport.

As the family was gathering in St. Ann's after the burial, one person who was noticeably absent was Louis Walker's son-in-law Davis Robinson. His wife, Suzanne, was quite concerned.

Davis quietly slipped into the pew next to her after the service had begun. In recounting why he was late, he explained to his wide-eyed wife that while leaving the cemetery, he became disoriented while driving and drove his car into an open grave. When Davis called AAA in Kennebunk to explain what he had done, they laughed hysterically and brought their entire fleet out to rescue him. Fortunately they got the car out right before the family of the person who was about to be buried arrived.

Davis's daughter Gracyn described the event as her father "driving himself to an early grave."

UP FROM THE GROUND

Another favorite funeral story involves my friend and colleague the Reverend Dr. Vienna Cobb Anderson. Vienna was the rector of St. Margaret's Church in Washington, DC. She is quite tall and statuesque, with flaming red hair, and is known for her very particular and exquisite taste in vestments.

While still a seminarian, Vienna was officiating at a gravesite in Washington's historic Rock Creek Cemetery, a beautiful cemetery with steep, dramatic views of the city. She was negotiating her way around that fake green grass they put around graves when she stepped in the wrong place and fell under the coffin into the grave. The undertakers grabbed her as she was clinging to the coffin. The Reverend Billy Shand, a friend and colleague, later asked if the family joined in singing the hymn "Up from the Grave *She* Arose"!

I Can Rhyme Too!

From time to time people with no religious affiliation to St. Columba's would call to see if we could help with a funeral. Gawler's Funeral Home is several blocks from the church, and one day they called to see if one of the clergy might be available to officiate at a funeral in their chapel. I agreed to go and brought my fellow assistant, Elisa Wheeler, because she had yet to officiate at a funeral and asked if she could come along.

When we got there, we met the daughter and son of the woman who had died. The daughter greeted us warmly, as did the son, who spoke in rhyme. I was a bit surprised, but the rhyme was very clever. We then proceeded into the chapel. After the service the daughter thanked us, as did the son, who again spoke in rhyme. I decided I would try my hand at it, and while I was composing out loud, Elisa poked me in the side. As we were leaving, she said, "He has a psychiatric condition and only speaks in rhyme!"

It Didn't Work

Sheila Lindveit and Anona Fowler were the parish secretaries. As any clergyperson will tell you, you're only as good as the parish secretaries make you out to look, and with a parish as large as St. Columba's with five clergy and over one thousand parishioners, Sheila and Anona kept things well in hand.

One day I walked in the office and said something, but got absolutely no response from either one of them. I decided I would feign illness and fall down on the floor between their desks, which faced one another. Without saying a word, they both stopped typing for a moment, peered over their desks, made eye contact with each other, and went right on typing.

Uh Oh!

In anticipation of the church building a columbarium, we stored people's ashes in the storeroom, where we kept everything from copy paper to ladders to cases of Communion wine. I went in one day to find something, and to get to whatever it was I was looking for, I shoved a bunch of boxes aside.

Later that day, someone went in to find Margaret's husband's ashes, which had been carefully placed by Louise. When it came time to inter his ashes, we *thought* we had found the right box . . .

The Meeting Gene

The Reverend Louise Lusignan, the rector's assistant, was the first person I ever heard use the term "meeting gene." Some people have it, and some do not.

St. Columba's was holding a regional meeting of the diocese when a woman sitting in the front row started to cry. Bishop Walker asked her if he could do something to help.

"I'm so sorry," she said, "but this is the most boring meeting I have ever attended."

"You're absolutely right," the bishop replied. "This meeting is adjourned."

The Front Lines

While at St. Columba's I began to realize that some of the pastoral situations that presented themselves were way beyond me. In some cases children and adults became "regular customers," and I would become concerned that their issues weren't heading toward any sort of resolution. I could offer love and acceptance, which was deeply appreciated and in many cases healing, but I couldn't offer much else.

I also realized parishioners and students felt seeing "the minister" did not hold the stigma that seeing a psychologist or psychiatrist might. I understood that line of thinking well because before I got myself into therapy, I felt the same way. But if they trusted me, perhaps they would be less threatened by that prospect.

To help me judge each situation while at St. Columba's, I began a weekly consultation with Dr. Lawrence Brain, Director of Adolescent Medicine at the Psychiatric Institute of Washington. Each week Elisa Wheeler, my associate at St. Columba's, and I would bring case studies to Larry and he would help us determine whether we could handle it or if it would be best to refer them to a professional. I tried as best I could to improve my diagnostic skills, but don't fancy myself as any kind of "therapist."

Over the course of my years—along with the regular responsibilities that go along with parish and school duties such as teaching, preaching, and officiating at weddings, baptisms, and funerals—I have encountered depression, bipolar disorder, anxiety disorder, obsessive-compulsive disorder, anorexia, bulimia, drug and alcohol addiction, physical and sexual abuse, along with just plain ol' sadness.

A lot of folks think ministers only work on Sundays!

Larry helped us to realize that as ministers we were, as he put it, "on the front lines" and that bears with it a lot of responsibility. I continued regular consultations while at St. Albans and now at the Episcopal School of Los Angeles.

TRIP TO IONA

While at St. Columba's, Bill Tully led a trip to the Island of Iona in Scotland. It is where Saint Columba reportedly landed and began converting the Scots after he sailed from Ireland, and is also where a number of the Scottish kings are buried.

I was so captivated by the history, beauty, and mystery of "The Holy Isle," I spent two summers there living at the Episcopal house and taking a crack at the contemplative life. What I discovered is that it really wasn't for me, except in small doses.

I wrote the following piece in the St. Columba's newsletter:

To the Parish . . .
The Trappist Monk and contemplative writer Thomas Merton has an impassioned dialogue with The Almighty at the conclusion of his

book The Seven Storey Mountain. *His autobiography is a gripping account of his wrestling with the contemplative life, a life with which I confess I have been wrestling. Hence the trip to Iona, a far cry from a Trappist Monastery, yet an environment that fostered a restlessness, a spiritual restlessness which caught me by surprise. Craig Eder told me it would be unlike anything I might expect.*

I guess I had expected peace and calm. I couldn't leave it all behind. I thought I could but it came with me. I couldn't escape it. I was foolish to think I could. It is my life . . . the same face looking back at me in the tiny mirror of my room with all the things that go along with it.

The contemplative life means to begin to wonder what you're doing with it . . . your life . . . your things. Physical and mental things. My contemplative life didn't begin on Iona, but Iona helped me to understand a little of what Thomas Merton was wrestling with when he faced some "things" with which we fill our lives—looking for meaning in them yet they distance us from God.

From one who has a lot of things . . . may you desire only those things in which you can see God, realizing that even then you may be called to give them up. They may be persons, places, or possessions, but in their being may they have shortened the distance between you and God, and may you rejoice in having had them.

GIANTS ON THE EARTH

I met the Reverend Craig Eder when we were assistants together at St. Columba's. He had many years earlier been chaplain of St. Albans School. I always told Craig I wanted to be like him when I "grew up." At the time we met, I hadn't a clue I would later have his old job.

Rowan LeCompte, the famous stained glass artisan responsible for many of the windows in the Washington National Cathedral, told me he attributed the enormous popularity of *The Hobbit* in the United States to Craig. He used the book in his religion classes at St. Albans. Orcs, evil characters in the book, appear in several of the windows Rowan designed in the school's Little Sanctuary depicting the trial of Saint Alban.

Craig and Edie Eder on their dory, *The George Cleaves*,
Clapboard Island, Maine

Along with his teaching and pastoral responsibilities, Craig took the students on many bike trips to Europe and Africa. He inspired the children to lives of service. His former students were devoted to him.

Toward the end of his time at St. Albans, shortly before he came to St. Columba's, he married Edith Gilliss, a widow with three children. They lived in a house in Cathedral Heights during the school year. Summers were spent in Maine, a tradition they continued into retirement.

Among the many things he did at St. Columba's was to lead a Bible study once a week called "The Seekers," which preceded Sargent House. I remember sitting in my office hearing them laugh their heads off.

Craig was gentle and kind and regarded as a "saint" by all who knew him. Except for one person—his wife. Edie was worried he would begin to believe it about himself, and she would have none of that!

We rarely saw Edie at St. Columba's. She was very much involved in her church, St. Stephen and the Incarnation in downtown DC. They had a very active social-action ministry, and from time to time she would go to demonstrations. Craig would remind her to "take your credit card" just in case she had to post bail.

Craig and Edie both grew up children of privilege, although Edie's fortune far exceeded Craig's. Her grandfather was Samuel F. Houston of Philadelphia and her great-grandfather was Henry Howard Houston, a director of the Pennsylvania Railroad and developer of Chestnut Hill.

Upon the death of her mother, Edith Houston Brown, Edie inherited Clapboard Island in Maine, just off the coast in Falmouth Foreside. Along with it came a forty-room mansion, which Edie's grandfather built at the turn of the century. They sold the mansion and half the island and kept the other half, where they built a stunning contemporary home designed by a St. Albans alumnus.

Now, mind you, with what they inherited they could have lived a very different sort of life, but when you walked into either of their homes, you'd think they invented shabby chic. They were New Englanders through and through and spent their money sensibly. They were extraordinarily generous to various charities anonymously.

They had no electricity on the island. At one time Edie's mother was told by the electric company it would cost fifty thousand dollars to send an electric line out there. She thought it was too much. They did have propane and a generator they ran once a day for the plumbing. The light came from Coleman lanterns and candles. There was no phone. Any correspondence had to be by letter, though from time to time Craig would arrange for a call from a pay phone in Falmouth. In their later years Edie did get a cell phone so she could "call out" if there was an emergency; otherwise, the phone was turned off. They used a dory to row themselves back and forth to the island.

Craig would buy his clothes from Goodwill or from outlets in Freeport. One year Edie's son John told me that once when his mother met him at the airport, she was wearing one red shoe and one blue shoe because "the others had worn out and these were perfectly fine." One winter a barge pulled up and burglars stole all the valuables from the house, which included original Stickley mission furniture, many antiques and paintings, and an extremely valuable nautical figurehead that washed up on the island years ago.

They took all the children and grandchildren on a cruise around the world with the money from the insurance.

I spent many summer weeks with them on the island with their assortment of dogs and my dog, Scruffy. One summer, when I took a summer rectorship and had to live in a very fancy house, Scruffy stayed with them. Craig said, "I guess that says something about our house!" Scruffy is now buried in his favorite spot amid the pine trees on Clapboard Island.

I remember a sermon Craig once gave. It began with a passage from the book of Genesis. "There was a time when giants ruled the earth . . ." He continued on speaking of the "giants" in his life at St. Columba's. The founding members of St. Columba's . . . the folks from Sargent House and "The Seekers" who were no longer with us, Esther Barr, Helen Pettit, the Fletchers, the Baggotts . . .

Now all of them, including Craig and Edie, are "giants" to me.

RAMER

At eighty-six, Ramer Simpson is currently the oldest and longest-serving volunteer at St. Columba's. The eight o'clock service could not begin without him. He opens the doors, folds the programs, makes the coffee, and ushers during the service.

The other essential thing he does is oversee the shortbread baking. St. Columba's is known nationwide for its delicious shortbread, and orders for Christmas begin in the late summer.

To say he is a character is an understatement. Everyone loves Ramer, with the possible exception of a former rector with whom he saw nothing eye to eye. During one particular heated exchange, Ramer informed the rector, "I'll outlast you and if I don't, I'll be out in the columbarium aggravating the hell out of you."

That rector is gone. Ramer is still greeting folks at the eight o'clock.

Zazu

Over the course of a year, the names read out loud on St. Columba's Sunday-morning parish prayer list come and go. One year one particular name stood out: Zazu. Maybe it was because her name was so unusual in the list with the Johns and the Marys and the Susans.

After about a year of being on the list, her name came up in the liturgy meeting. Anona Fowler, a parish secretary, remembered that a woman named Barbara had called and asked for Zasu to be put on the list. No one knew Barbara or Zazu, and it was decided to take her name off.

The next Sunday after the service, Anona was walking out of church with her son Perry. She had been wondering whether or not Perry had been paying attention in church, but then he asked, "Mom, what happened to Zazu?"

In fact, that Sunday just about everyone asked the same thing.

The staff of St. Columba's

The Call to Be a School Chaplain

I don't think I ever learned anything very well until I had to teach it to someone else . . . at least that's what I was thinking when I went to see Bishop John T. Walker to tell him I thought I wanted to move from parish ministry to be a school chaplain. It seemed to square with where I was finding my vocation, working particularly with young people. But in all honesty, I've learned many adults have forgotten, or never got the message, that they too are loved for who they are. It's a message worth repeating over and over despite your age.

I had been at St. Columba's for four years and, although I loved the folks there, I thought being in an academic environment would give me the time I needed to learn some things I *should* have learned in seminary. As you might have gleaned from an earlier chapter, I was pretty over-whelmed while there. By this time, however, I did understand that there was more than one woman named Mary in the Bible (though I'm still not quite sure what to do with the Apocrypha).

After my meeting with Bishop Walker and following interviews, Headmaster Mark Mullin offered me a job as chaplain to the Lower School at St. Albans. I was to teach Hebrew scriptures to the C Form (4th grade), New Testament to the B Form (5th grade), Cathedral Faith to the 6th grade, Ethics to the 8th grade, and Philosophy of Religion to the 11th grade. On top of that, I was to preach in Lower and Upper School chapel—piece of cake! (*Are you kidding?*)

I owe Mark an enormous debt of gratitude. It was a job that for twenty-five years brought me great joy.

Farewell to the People of St. Columba's

Dear People of St. Columba's,
I am sitting at my new desk in my new office at St. Albans writing this thank you "note." To my left on the wall (so I can see it while I'm on the phone) is a collage of pictures of my life with you at St. Colum-ba's. I have the briefcase that the vestry gave me at my feet (crammed with half graded papers and books). On top of my file cabinet behind me is a picture of the staff of St. Columba's (the women look the same,

the men have experienced a slight hair loss) and scattered around office and home are mementos of my life with you, not to mention a lot more money in my savings. Thank you! It reminds me of the discretionary fund my Dad gave me when I went to college. I feel like a kid his first time away from home. You should have seen me walking out the front door on the first day of school with shoes shined and briefcase in hand!

Some years ago, Bill Tully and I remarked to one another we felt we were called to St. Columba's in order to "grow up." Well, folks, you did your job, and I hope I did too and now I'm on my way. I remain eternally grateful for all the love and support I received at "home" with you.

There is a funny little rectangular window in this new office, and it looks out into the hall. Through it I can see kids going to class, from class, and skipping class. They knock on the window, make faces at me (so do the faculty), they wave at me, and sometimes the hall is empty. It is a window to this new world, and it is wonderful, a world where I am surrounded by all of you and thoughts of love. A world where love looks back at me with braces on its teeth or a nose pressed up against the glass or from a desk in room 101.

Speaking of room 101, I have to be there in a couple of minutes . . .

I will be seeing you as a fellow parishioner, friend, and occasional preacher and teacher.

Thank you from the bottom of my heart for all that you have done. Come see me in my new world. I'm the one in the lower school hallway behind the glass.

Will

St. Albans School

THE FIRST DAY

I SPENT THE SUMMER PREPARING MY LESSON PLANS FOR ST. ALBANS (STA), and by the first day I was ready to go. So at eight o'clock, as I was in my office organizing my day, Paul Herman, the head of the Lower School, appeared at my door and said, "Will, we have a little problem . . . Richard Case has run away."

Richard, after his parents' divorce, had come to live with his father and stepmother in Washington, DC, and even though his older brother Eddie was with him and enrolled in the Upper School, he was having none of it. So right after his father dropped him off, he took off for God-knows-where . . . and it fell upon me to find him. I spent a good part of the morning searching for him on the Cathedral Close, which with its gardens has many possible hiding places.

Fortunately, I found him. Neither of us can quite remember where. I couldn't remember what I said or how I tried to reason with him, but Richard remembered distinctly. He said I said to him, "Richard, this is *my* first day too!" Which at the time did not make one bit of difference to him.

I missed all my classes that day. Fortunately, I was not reprimanded in any way for my absences. Little did we know then what would unfold in Richard's life and how we would bond as I faced with him the death of his brother Eddie from leukemia.

I still have a card Eddie sent me shortly before he died. It has a picture of Jack Nicholson on the front from *One Flew Over the Cuckoo's Nest*. In it he thanked me for taking care of Richard.

Richard now lives in New York with his wife, Megan, and is the father of three boys.

That first day taught me what life really is about. In spite of our best-laid plans, it's about being lost . . . and found.

Incidentally, on his first day of kindergarten, Richard and Megan's eldest boy refused to go to school.

LEARNING TO TEACH

Until St. Albans, I had never taught in a formal academic setting. I had overseen discussions in youth groups a zillion times, but I'll be honest and say church history was never one of my strongest subjects.

My first year of teaching in 1985 was challenging enough, but then the boys, of course, had to test me. I remember two boys questioning me about independent sources, which are sources other than the Gospels that refer to the historical figure of Jesus. I replied I guess I might have learned it once, but that I couldn't remember.

They both said rather sarcastically, "You don't know?"

Let's just say I'll never forget the names Tacitus and Josephus.

Despite that initiation, I had a lot of fun teaching and they had fun with me. Over the years, I acquired the nickname "Reverend Fun," which I *think* was a compliment.

That first year was a doozy. In another class the boys discovered that while I was writing on the blackboard and my back was to them, one of the boys could sneak up and flip the pages of my notes with a pen so I'd be confused as to what I had just gone over.

Another time, again while my back was turned, a spitball fight like no other took place until I got wise by seeing all the paper wads on the floor. The next day, having concealed a camera, I snapped a picture of the perpetrators, one with an open umbrella to protect himself.

Throughout my years at STA, my Philosophy of Religion course in the Upper School had many nicknames. My favorite was "Philo with Billow." One of my students, Casey, added "bring a pillow." Ha ha.

Thanks to Mixy back in seminary, I learned that religious education is at its best when religious dogma is met with a healthy dose of skepticism. In one of my classes, when I asked the students if they wanted proof of the existence of God, most hands went up except for a few boys, one of whom said, "I don't. It would be like being brain dead. Life wouldn't be very interesting."

The Filioque Clause

You cannot come to know and experience the Good News if you are put to sleep by theological minutia.
—Walter Thorne

Headmaster Vance Wilson once called me into his office to be interviewed by a very earnest young graduate student in theology at a prestigious university. He asked me something like, "How did you approach with your students the controversy over the filioque clause?" I looked at him like, *Are you kidding?* I glanced at Vance, who was sitting to the side working at his computer, and I could see a big grin on his face. It was a setup.

I told our visitor the truth . . . It was all I could do to get the kids to remember "Jesus loves me." We never got to the filioque clause, the controversy that separated the Eastern and Western Orthodox Churches. I tried the Council of Nicaea once. Not a big hit. While we had an extensive curriculum at St. Albans, we tried to be practical with the time allowed. I really just wanted them to be curious and understand how best to study scripture.

I always tried to have fun with the kids. By the end of my time at St. Albans, because of pastoral responsibilities I was only teaching one class, which the kids called "God Class." I tested out a lot of books and movies over the years to see what seemed to work. Books that were big hits included *A Prayer for Owen Meany* by John Irving, *Wishful Thinking: A Seeker's ABC* by Frederick Buechner, and *Meeting Jesus Again for the First Time* by Marcus Borg. Required papers were meant to be reflective. Among the most meaningful were the ones in which I asked the students to write about a time when an illusion you had about life was dispelled and you saw how life really is, because if your concept of God isn't grounded in reality, it isn't going to do you much good.

By far the most popular part of the curriculum were the movies (no surprise): *Monty Python's Life of Brian, Dogma, Religulous, The Exorcist, Saved,* and *Jesus Camp.* All of which at least got them thinking.

STREAM OF CONSCIOUSNESS

It didn't take long for the kids to figure out that it didn't take much to get me to digress from the subject at hand. I would have a lesson plan, but the truth is if the kids found it boring, I probably did too. While I was in high school, after a lengthy conversation Ruth Johnson and I would retrace what we had just talked about to try to figure out how we ended up where we did. It actually is a very good memory and teaching tool.

THE DEVIL

My introduction to Satan was watching the film *The Exorcist* while in college. I went to see it with a bunch of my fraternity brothers, and we were freaked out for weeks. Although the night after we saw it, we did hide under one of the brother's beds and moved it up and down, recalling one of the famous scenes from the movie. He didn't appreciate it.

I would explain the church's teachings to my students and tell them they take it very seriously. Together we would read the baptismal service, in which people are required to "renounce Satan and all the spiritual forces of wickedness that rebel against God." Then I would actually show *The Exorcist* to the students (I can't believe no parents ever complained). Along with that we would read the firsthand accounts of the events described by the diarist in an article I discovered in the *Washingtonian.*

One night while having dinner at the Cosmos Club with the Right Reverend Hayes Rockwell, the Episcopal Bishop of Missouri, I told him about my course and asked him if he had ever had an occasion to appoint an exorcist. He said, "As a matter of fact, I just did." He asked me to send him copies of everything I was using in my course.

Another person who took accounts of exorcisms very seriously was my friend the late M. Scott Peck, MD, author of *The Road Less Traveled* and *People of the Lie.* He believed he witnessed evil in his patients that might only be attributed to possession by the devil.

Whether you believe in Satan or not, I felt a responsibility to teach about him. After all, Jesus not only talked *about* him, but *to* him.

UNDERSTANDING THE LITURGY

We would reenact liturgies of the church such as baptisms, weddings, and funerals with the hope that the kids would begin to realize the power of the promises they might someday choose to make. The students would volunteer to be brides and grooms and attendants. We'd have doll babies to baptize with parents and godparents, and when it came time to have a funeral, we would eulogize one of the kids in the class. These particular classes were always full of fun. The kids would scream with laughter imagining having to marry their classmates. One year my assistant Sally Bartlett stood in to "marry" a student. They referred to one another as husband and wife until he graduated.

A BIRTHDAY SURPRISE

For many years my classes included students from the National Cathedral School for Girls. One year on my birthday, unbeknownst to me, the girls in the class hired an entertainer to come to the classroom and deliver a singing telegram.

He arrived in the doorway . . . wearing what appeared to be long underwear, a diaper, and red tennis shoes. He shot a rubber-tipped arrow at the blackboard, picked up his boom box, jumped over a desk between two of the boys, and dropped the boom box on my desk. He then pushed the play button and sang a couple of songs, one of which I believe was "Happy Birthday to You."

He left as quickly as he arrived. The girls were hysterical with laughter—I only wish you could have seen the looks on the boys' faces. One of them said to me afterward, "Mr. Billow, I was *really* scared." And I think he really was. So was I.

There is a picture of the entertainer posing with Jack McCune, the assistant headmaster, in the yearbook that year.

SHOW-AND-TELL

One thing I had the kids do in my classes is tell funny stories from their childhood, and this one took the cake: We were talking about whether any of us had show-and-tell in the classroom when we were little. Of course, everyone did, and we went around the room recalling the special thing we brought.

When we got to Lily, she explained they had show-and-tell in her nursery school class at St. Columba's (where I had been chaplain), and as they went around the classroom, one poor little girl could not find what she brought. It was her brand-new Barbie, and she was beside herself.

The teacher turned the classroom upside down to find it. When she could not, the teacher explained that by the end of the day if anyone "found" the missing Barbie, they could leave it on her desk. Sadly, the Barbie never showed up.

Lily still has it.

THE SEVEN DWARFS

In my classes we would discuss fairy tales and how many of them seek to describe aspects of our personalities. I would always have the kids try to name all of the dwarfs from *Snow White and the Seven Dwarfs.* One particular day we got through almost all of them—Sleepy, Dopey, Grumpy, Happy, Doc, Bashful—when one of the boys yelled out "Horny!" Unfortunately, the director of admissions had just opened the door, giving a tour to prospective parents. I'm not sure if they sent their son to STA or not.

Incidentally, the correct answer is Sneezy.

"GOOD MORNING, KID, AND WELCOME TO REALITY"

In his book *Dynamics of Faith,* author Paul Tillich discusses the importance of symbols in our lives. According to Tillich, we don't choose them, but rather they choose us. We simply respond. Symbols are words, stories, objects, and rituals that lead us to what Tillich calls our "ultimate concern," which we might also call God. He also speaks of doubt being an essential element of faith. Likewise, Frederick Buechner says, "Doubt is the ants in the pants of faith."

What you don't want to do is respond to a symbol that won't get you to your ultimate concern, or else you'll experience "existential disappointment." An example might be your own physical beauty, which undoubtedly will fade. Another might be putting all your faith in a person who disappoints you or in being rich and then losing your shirt in the stock market.

I found this an invaluable discussion with the kids, as they are bombarded with symbols every day of their lives, but part of growing up is learning from the mistakes we make along the way.

I had the students write what I called an "epiphany paper" about a time in their lives when an illusion was dispelled and life became real to them. Following a particular faith or philosophy of life doesn't really do you any good unless it deals with what's really going on in your life. In one paper one of the boys wrote about discovering one of his parents was having an affair. He concluded it by writing, "Good morning, kid, and welcome to reality."

WRITING THEIR OWN THEOLOGY

For their final assignment in Philo, I had the kids "write their own theology." The word *gospel* means "good news." Just as the Gospels recount the life of Jesus and why people believed in him, I would ask my students the question, "If someone were to be a follower of you, what would they have to believe? What would be the 'good news' of believing in you?" The question prompted wonderful papers where I would discover the things in which they found meaning: books, movies, television shows, people, poems, and so forth. The one thing they were not allowed at the end was to be deemed "a shallow person," which made them laugh and then, of course, they would accuse one another of being that person.

Here is a poem written by a former student, Gideon, at the conclusion of a semester in Philo:

The Tao of Pooh . . . the how of you . . .
Tillichian Philo perceived by Billow . . . Equus . . .
Alan Strang was quite a strain,
But "horse sense," perception, a notion

Of what is odder; became grist for the
Mill and fodder!!!

Will we ever appreciate all that was
"Meany"? He will live in my heart
Calmly and seemly . . . He is "pointing"
This moment to Kuwait and Saudi,
In me he is questioning Messers.
Bush, Baker, and Cheney.

Constructing a life that has virtue
And message invites views from Teilhard,
Toynbee, Miller and Graham,
All with great effort to know who I am.

There are many questions and few self-replies
But I look in a mirror with opened eyes . . .
What do I see there and hear in prayer?
A young man with hope and vision and heart
Who will struggle and study to learn his part.
If the part is jumbled and muddy, unclear . . .
If I keep reading and thinking it should be clear.

A life philosophy seems like a cinch until you wonder.
That is quite the key to getting down and under.
It's under your skin and under your rib . . .
Next to your heart that you wander and wonder.
Magnanimous, well informed, a conscience that cares.
Generous, confident, honest and stately;
Loving family, serving Church, giving heart to duty.
Sorting it out; making it work; struggle tomorrow
With light and dark . . . This is what Philo has come
To mean . . . and without Billow it would all go unseen.

Gideon is now an Episcopal priest, formerly chaplain of the Episcopal High School in Alexandria, Virginia, and now rector of St. John's
Episcopal Church in Cold Spring Harbor, New York.

Scratch 'n' Sniff

Brendan and Lila Sullivan have been friends of mine for many years. Their boys, Teddy and Brendan Jr., attended St. Albans, and I officiated at both of their weddings and the baptisms of their children. Brendan Sr. is a prominent Washington attorney, perhaps best known for representing Lieutenant Colonel Oliver North during the Iran-Contra scandal, which gripped the nation in 1987. During the hearings, Brendan objected to some of the questions being posed to Colonel North as to his involvement. At one point during the questioning, Joint House Select Committee chairman Senator Daniel Inouye suggested Colonel North just speak for himself. Brendan famously replied, "Well, sir, I am not a potted plant."

Mostly I knew Brendan as a devoted dad, attending his boys' ball games and serving on St. Albans' Governing Board. He was deeply committed to raising faculty salaries, as the cost of living in DC was getting very high.

Several years ago, Brendan Sr. and I ran into each other on the train from New York to DC. We sat together and chatted while we worked—he on some legal brief and I grading papers, which I then stuffed into my leather satchel. When we got to Washington, he very kindly gave me a ride home.

After dinner, I was taking my papers out of my satchel to enter the grades in my grade book and realized they were all wet. When I looked in the bottom of the bag, I realized a bottle I had taken to New York had opened and my papers had been soaking in vodka. The problem was, I had to hand them back to the kids! I also kind of wondered if Brendan could smell it.

I took all the papers out and scattered them around the living room to dry them out. Then, the next morning, I had my secretary, Sally Bartlett, "scratch 'n' sniff" each paper. Luckily she couldn't smell a thing and I could hand them back.

Everyone's a Believer

When the mother of one of our students died after a long illness, the entire football team rode the bus to attend her funeral, which was held at an evangelical church. In the midst of the service, the minister asked all those who "accepted the Lord Jesus Christ into their life" to raise their hands. If they didn't, they were encouraged to come down to the altar to pray with the minister. I looked out over the congregation, amused. Glancing left and right at their classmates and not wanting to be singled out, every single boy slowly raised his hand—Jews, Muslims, Buddhists, agnostics, even atheists. That day everyone was a believer.

ADAM, EVE, AND STEVE

Early in my tenure at St. Albans, I was trying to get the kids engaged and interested in moral decision-making. One way to do it (or so I thought at the time) was to open up topics for theological debate. I assumed it would be done in a thoughtful and respectful manner if it was done during chapel . . . big mistake. Sometimes boys just can't help themselves.

One day a year St. Albans has what is called "diversity day." It is a day devoted to a particular topic, and one year the topic the kids and their advisors picked was homosexuality. *Perfect.*

As I recall, chapel began as usual with a hymn and a reading. I introduced the topic for discussion, saying something boring like it being an issue in the Episcopal Church with regard to acceptance, inclusion, and, as remote as it seemed, maybe even same-sex marriage. Then I opened the topic up for discussion. The boys at St. Albans are never shy about expressing their opinions.

It began pretty well, and several of the boys spoke. I remember a senior saying something really thoughtful. Following that, another boy stood up and said, "Well, as far as I'm concerned, God made Adam and Eve, *not* Adam and Steve!" The whole place erupted in laughter. Whatever meaningful conversation I had intended went out the window and it was time for sports.

Regardless of the outcome of that particular chapel, at least it began a dialogue. Over the next several years, the boys created a Gay-Straight Alliance with the girls from the National Cathedral School (NCS). A number of boys felt it a safe enough environment to "come out" to the student body and bring their dates to the prom. We now have transgender alumni.

Several years later I realized we had come a long way when planning for diversity day. When I asked the diversity committee if they wanted homosexuality to be one of the topics, a number of kids said, "Oh Reverend Billow, do we have to talk about it *again*?! It's just not an issue for us."

I do have to confess that although I believe the vast majority of the St. Albans community are supportive of gay marriage and lifestyle, some students, parents, and faculty are not, though they generally do not express their displeasure publicly. One faculty member said to me privately, "I hope there's still room for me here." I was taken aback . . . I certainly hadn't wanted to help create an environment where someone did not feel welcome. There still needed to be respect and inclusion regardless your point of view.

THE THREE BEST REASONS TO BE A TEACHER

I've been told any number of times that "the three best reasons to be a teacher are June, July, and August." I do try to take advantage of the respite summer provides. I spend a good part of my summer in Small Point, Maine.

In the mid-1980s my former fieldwork supervisor at St. Francis Episcopal Church in Potomac, Maryland, the Reverend Almus Thorp, asked if I would help sail his boat from its dry dock in Bath, Maine, to his cottage in Boothbay Harbor. I jumped at the chance. Having also been invited to Maine by St. Columba friends Alaster and Sue MacDonald, I could then visit them in Small Point, which is about forty-five minutes south of Boothbay by car, shorter by boat.

Just as Almus and I sailed out of the New Meadows River into the ocean, a thick fog rolled in. I think it was then that Almus informed me his compass didn't work. We sailed for hours heeding the sound of bell buoys to keep us from crashing into the surrounding rocks. Almus brought a bag of Cheetos and a bottle of Jack Daniels up from below, and that helped our nerves somewhat. By some miracle, when the fog began to lift we weren't miles out to sea but actually found ourselves in Boothbay Harbor.

I left Almus in the early evening when it was still light and made my way to Bath. I took Route 1 south, and once over the bridge at Bath, turned left at the Bath Iron Works on the road to Small Point.

Hamilton Leithauser with Mebane on the porch in Small Point
PHOTO COURTESY OF BRYAN LEITHAUSER

Because the folks who live there guard their privacy so carefully, Small Point is hard to find. Luckily, I had explicit instructions to the Small Point Club from Alaster and found the anchor on the side of the road, where I was to turn left on Club Road. The sign was hidden by the trees, as are most of the road signs in Small Point.

It was beginning to get dark when just past the tennis court on my left I saw the club. It sat high above the ocean and was surrounded by beautiful gardens. I pulled up in front, parked, and walked up to the front door. I knocked and a waiter in a tuxedo welcomed me and asked if I would like a cocktail. I thought to myself, "This is my kind of club!"

I ordered a drink, and as I waited for him to return to show me to my room, a lovely woman appeared. She introduced herself as Elena Vandervoort and welcomed me. I assumed she was the manager, so I introduced myself and told her that I was embarrassed to be dressed the way I was, as I had been sailing. I hadn't shaved or combed my hair and was in a T-shirt and jeans, but promised I would be more presentable after I got to my room. She looked a little startled, then laughed and said, "Oh dear, this isn't the club. This is my home. The club is several houses down on the left. We happen to be having a fundraising event here tonight, and I assumed you were one of the guests!"

The waiter brought me my drink, which Elena insisted I finish. Totally embarrassed, I quickly drank my drink, thanked Elena for being so gracious, and left before any of her guests arrived and made my way to the club.

Elena and her late husband, Peter, were to become some of my dearest friends.

The truth is, to be lost and confused about where you are in Small Point is easy to do. People are always asking directions because nothing is carefully marked. Many years ago, friends Dottie and Ernie Fuller from New Canaan arrived at the house they had rented from their friends Kennon and Sabra Jayne and found the doors locked. They climbed in the window, got the sheets out of the dryer (standard for Small Point), made dinner, and went to bed. The next morning they woke up and made breakfast, and at noon the real renters arrived. They had spent the night in the wrong house!

The Small Point Club community sits atop a cliff on the waterfront surrounded by several immense clapboard houses built around the turn of the last century. Just south of Popham Beach, at low tide you can walk a sandy beach for six miles between Cape Small and Fort Popham, which is most unusual considering Maine's generally rocky coastline. While there, your life revolves around the tides. If you don't time your walk on the beach carefully, chances are you'll have to swim back to the club—which has happened to me on occasion. The views are spectacular. Just below the club, what is left of the wreck of the *Willard* still protrudes from the sand.

For many years a Sunday morning service has traditionally been held on the porch at the club, which sits high above the ocean overlooking the beach. If I am fortunate enough to be in Small Point on a Sunday, I will officiate. We have to dust off the prayer books and hymnals we find on the bookshelves in the club, all of which date from 1928. I have officiated at several baptisms and memorials there that have meant a great deal to the residents and their families. The "Navy Hymn" is always a must.

For several years I rented the Hoffman house right next to the club. The way I came about this was due to the generosity of the man who built it, Fenno Hoffman, chair of the English Department at the Rhode Island School of Design.

One year while staying at the club, four of my students from St. Albans called and said they were on their way to Mount Desert Island and wanted to stop and see me. They drove all night to get there, arriving in a 1975 Volkswagen van after speeding down Club Road at six o'clock in the morning. I believe they were first apprehended for speeding by Nancy Chandler. Shirley McComb, then the club manager and a graduate of NCS, arranged for them to stay at the club, of course on my nickel. At that time the club had rather strict rules on behavior and dress, still requiring jackets for dinner—not exactly the place for four recent STA graduates on a toot. When Fenno heard of this, he came over and told me he was going away for a week, and why didn't I just move over to his house and bring the kids?

The kids stayed a little longer than expected, I think because they were overwhelmed by the beauty of Small Point. Between Small Point and Popham is what is known as the Bates-Morse Mountain Conservation Area, a six-hundred-acre gift of the St. John family to Bates College. It is an important area ecologically, with salt marshes along the Sprague River, protected nesting areas in the dunes, and fantastic rock formations jutting up out of the ground.

The boys had a ball boating, fishing, and surfing. I remember one of the graduates in particular, Patrick Flaherty, spending hours on the beach just gazing up at the terns and plovers swirling around him. He had been introduced to birding in Bob Hahn's B Form (5th grade) class and would accompany Bob every year on the White House Bird Count. He became a forestry major in college.

Former student Hamilton Leithauser comes every summer with his wife, Anna, and their children, as do Anna and Hugh McIntosh and their kids. STA parents Bryan and Mark Leithauser now rent Fenno's house for their entire family. We used to rent the house together, but because they now have four grandchildren under the age of six, I rent what's known as Sydney Smith House, named for a late grande dame of Small Point, which happens to be just a stone's throw from the Vandervoorts, where I made that fateful wrong turn many years ago.

A New Chapel Model

I have to confess, I never liked it much when I had to come up with several chapels a week. And let's face it, who wants to listen to the same person all the time? Certainly not teenage boys.

Then in the 1990s two remarkable chapels happened, one right after the other, that got me off the hook. I haven't regretted it one minute.

We had an elected vestry with a senior warden who could have been starring in an episode of *Glee*. He was the co-captain of the football team and had the lead in that year's musical. Early on in the season, he quit the team. I can't recall his reasons, but suffice it to say, it shocked the team, the coaches, and the entire community. In a place like St. Albans that celebrated sports, there was the danger of him being branded a "quitter."

A week or so later, he decided he'd made a mistake and wanted back on the team. They welcomed him back. He came to me and asked if he could give a chapel talk about it. I said of course, and knowing him as I did, I trusted it would be fine.

It was more than fine. It was about forgiveness. At the time, in a school such as St. Albans, boys weren't very comfortable about exposing their vulnerabilities. Mike spoke of being confused and making what he realized was a mistake. He spoke of his fear of not being accepted back, not so much by his coaches as by his teammates.

He received a standing ovation.

On the heels of that talk, Malcolm Lester, our lacrosse coach, asked if he could speak. I wasn't in the habit of vetting chapel talks, particularly by the faculty, so I was grateful and curious as to what Malcolm was going to say.

As he stood in front of 250 young men, he spoke of something he said he never had spoken of publicly before, but because of the love and support he felt at St. Albans, he wanted to share it. He said, "My mother is gay."

At the end of his chapel talk, he too received a standing ovation.

And so began at St. Albans the transformation of our Upper School chapels from being dominated by the clergy and faculty to being dominated by the boys, who because they appreciated the honesty of the speakers, took the brave steps of revealing who they really were to their classmates.

THE CHAPLAIN'S OFFICE

I have realized that many of the stories I have to tell about St. Albans I heard in my office when the children forgot I was sitting there. I generally would only interrupt their conversations when something concerned me.

My office was in the "new" wing (built in the 1960s). It was the first door on the left as you entered the building, with a huge window that looked out over the circle in front of the school. The circle is known as "Senior Circle," even though as long as I was at STA, no members of the senior class were ever allowed to park there.

In the center of the circle is the Glastonbury Thorn. Legend has it that when Saint Joseph of Arimathea founded the Abbey at Glastonbury in England, he planted his staff in the ground. The staff, made from the same tree as Jesus's crown of thorns, was said to have immediately bloomed. Our tree came from a shoot of that tree. Legend also has it that it blooms every time English royalty comes to Washington. The kids got a little nervous one year when it didn't appear to bloom when Queen Elizabeth was visiting, so one of the boys sneaked out and taped daisies on it.

From my office I could see all the comings and goings at the school, and they could also see me. There wasn't much privacy. If I needed to, I could always shut my door, but that signaled something serious because my door was almost always open. So, if I had to have a serious chat, I would generally leave the office. It was just easier.

I also had to be careful not to leave anything of a sensitive nature on my desk. My office floor was an obstacle course, generally filled with students, along with their backpacks, all kinds of sports equipment—lacrosse sticks, basketballs, soccer balls—shirts, ties, and basically anything they forgot at home that parents would have to drop off. Although it was pretty chaotic at times, I wouldn't have had it any other way.

Throughout the week, I would learn who was grounded by his parents, who had an unsupervised party, who was in trouble with what teacher, and who might simply be having a tough time. Some of the funniest things I heard were the kids' descriptions and impersonations of their teachers, my colleagues, whom I would almost always defend because I knew they would do the same for me.

Funny Kid Stories
The following are funny stories and situations involving the kids that could and did happen through the course of a given day.

The School Prayer
The St. Albans School Prayer has always been important to the students. For many years, students in the Lower School were required to memorize it. It is recited with regularity at alumni events and memorial services.

It, however, was never prayed more earnestly than it was one night by three St. Albans students in the late '80s.

The National Cathedral sits atop Mount St. Alban in Washington, DC, one of the highest points in the city. On the south side of the cathedral, at the foot of the south transept, are two sets of very steep steps. One set leads from the cathedral doors to Pilgrim Road below. The second set also leads down to Pilgrim Road as it winds down the hillside to the grounds of St. Albans School. Across Pilgrim Road at the very bottom of these steps is a magnificent bronze statue of George Washington riding on the famous racehorse Man o' War. The donor who had given the statue had said he wanted "the world's bestest man on the world's bestest horse!" The horse has agate eyes.

Late one evening, David and Vernon, both sons of alumni who also happened to be former and present Governing Board chairs, were driving on the Cathedral Close. They were joined by their good friend, David. At the time, to be chased by the Cathedral Police, also known as "the God Squad," was considered a sport. The three boys decided it would be fun to drive down the Pilgrim Road steps in Vernon's Chevy Tahoe, reciting the school prayer on a loudspeaker.

They turned off the road and headed down the second set of steps toward the statue of George Washington. Here is the St. Albans School Prayer, as printed on the school's website:

> *Vouchsafe thy blessing, we beseech thee, O Lord, upon this School and upon all other works undertaken in thy fear and for thy glory; and grant that all who serve thee here, whether as teachers or learners, may set thy holy will ever before them, and seek always to do such things as are pleasing in thy sight; that so both the Church and the Commonwealth of this land may benefit by their labors, and they themselves may attain unto everlasting life; through Jesus Christ our Lord. Amen.*

They made it. They did not get apprehended by the God Squad.

Miraculously, George Washington still rides Man o' War, agate eyes intact.

The Prayer List

One of the boys came into my office one day and sat down. I knew him to be particularly spiritual. He said he had a problem that was really troubling him. He told me when he said his prayers at night, he couldn't get through all of the people on his list without falling asleep.

I asked him, "How many people do you have on your list?"

He said, "Five hundred and thirty-two."

I suggested maybe he should break them into smaller groups, and then he could get to them all over the course of the week. I also told him I thought that God would understand. He seemed very relieved.

The Theological Society

I've had many nicknames over the years—Reverend Rev B, Reverendo, Willow—but maybe the most interesting was one that was conferred upon me by the STA Theological Society, Wise Old Red Beard.

The kids had to come up with a name for an organization that would look good on college recommendations, so they decided on Theological Society. Hamilton was the president. The society would meet in my office on Monday nights after sports and before they'd head home. The draw, of course, was pizza.

As we gathered in my office, a discussion would ensue that would go something like this:

Me (aka Wise Old Red Beard): "What should we talk about?"

Hamilton: "I don't know, Wise Old . . . Think of something."

One particular evening, we actually got into a discussion about Jesus, which was a miracle in itself, when Harry, a junior at STA and a "lifer" at the Cathedral Schools, who was listening rather intently, stopped the discussion:

Harry: "Wait a minute . . ."

Hamilton: "What?"

Harry: "You mean he really existed?"

Hamilton: "Who?"

Harry: "Jesus . . . You mean . . . He was an actual person?"

All of us: "*What?*"

When she heard about the discussion, Harry's aunt, my great friend and colleague Bryan Leithauser, quipped, "So much for being educated your whole life at the Cathedral Schools."

The Theological Society PHOTO COURTESY OF BRYAN LEITHAUSER

In an unrelated incident, Hamilton and Harry, not wanting to finish their assigned run in intramurals, decided to take the bus back to school from Ward Circle. When they got off the bus, they saw Jordan Contrato, who had a similar idea, get out of a cab.

"It Worked!"

Luke Russert, Yuri Anderson, Danny Zevnik, and one boy who will neither confirm nor deny his involvement, all seniors who should have been attending lunch, appeared in my office and reported they had been trying to shoot crows on telephone wires in Cathedral Heights with a BB gun.

Not surprisingly, as Cleveland Park is a neighborhood of rather large homes in close proximity to one another, one of the BBs went through the window of a house. They asked me, "What should we do?" I told them they should go to the flower shop and then go back to the house, give the lady who lives there the flowers, apologize, and tell her you'll pay for the window. They came back later that afternoon and said, "It worked!"

Luke told me later that, according to her husband, the poor woman had recently moved to DC from Belgium and the incident only reinforced what she had heard about American gun culture.

He Did What?

Several boys came racing into my office one day because one of their classmates had "pierced his wiener." I asked, "What am I supposed to do about it?" They just looked at me . . . then at one another . . . and left.

Later that week when the Theological Society was meeting for dinner, a platter of hot dogs appeared on the table. One had an earring.

It's Not as Bad as It Looks

Post 9-11, several boys driving around with towels on their heads were picked up by DC's finest after shooting girls from NCS with Super Soakers on Wisconsin Avenue from the back of an SUV. From my window, I could see police escorting one of them into the headmaster's office.

The boy, surrounded by four police officers, said to the headmaster's secretary, "Mrs. Grant, this isn't as bad as it looks!"

There followed a serious discussion about cultural sensitivity and how our lives changed after 9-11.

The Motorcycle

One morning, I got a call that one of the boys had wrecked his motorcycle on the corner of Woodley and Reno Roads. I raced out of the office to find that he was fine, but the motorcycle was not.

I first called his mother to report he was fine, but had wrecked his motorcycle. She replied, "He doesn't have a motorcycle." I then called his father. He too replied, "He doesn't have a motorcycle."

He had been hiding it at his grandmother's.

I Must Be Psychic!

A woman who lived in the neighborhood called to report that St. Albans students were smoking behind Alban Towers, which is across Wisconsin Avenue from the school. When I asked her how she knew it was our boys, she said, "Because they are wearing their St. Albans jackets." When I confronted the boys after chapel, they were incredulous: "How did you find out?!"

Similarly, several of them got arrested for drinking beer in Battery Kemble Park identified in the same way. A conversation followed about how the boys need to realize they represent the school when beyond the campus.

Things Overheard on the Way into Chapel

STA Upper Schooler eager to get to sports: "Oh sh*t! It's Communion."

STA Lower Schoolers on the way to my retirement service: "What's the service for?" asks one boy. "Oh, it's for some dead guy," another replies.

BEDLAM OF ECCENTRICITIES: THE FACULTY AND STAFF

My predecessor as chaplain, Roger Bowen, was fond of the quote that a great school contains a "bedlam of eccentricities," and that was certainly true of St. Albans. Hogwarts had nothing on us, particularly when it came to the faculty.

One of the things I miss the most, having retired, are my wonderful and brilliant colleagues. Bryan Leithauser, who for years served as our social service coordinator, suggested a book or play should be written titled *Burling Lounge*—the faculty lounge where we would gather and commiserate on a daily basis and generally laugh our heads off about situations that would present themselves over the course of our day.

We felt a loss when smoking in the lounge was banned, and Thierry Boussard, Henri Billey and Mariano Munoz (all members of the language department) could no longer join us between classes. But after their fix, they would come in and regale us with the ridiculosities of teaching very smart and clever boys. But let me tell you, the kids met their match when they tangled with each of them.

I miss the regular occurrence of memorable one-liners from faculty and students alike. It has been a joy to spend so much of my life surrounded by brilliant and funny people.

Mariano Munoz, who taught Spanish and economics, was fond of saying, when a boy did something about which he did not approve, "Of all the sperm in the universe, *yours* got through?" He was quick and a regular source of memorable lines:

- When asked by a rude ninth-grader, mid-lecture, "Señor, how many wives have you had?" Mariano responded with his own question, "My own or other people's?"
- While smoking outside his first-period classroom, he often responded to the greetings of his students by noting that he was "enjoying my vegetarian breakfast."
- While still smoking after his surgery for oral cancer, he responded to his concerned students by noting that he was "trying to smoke it out."
- While discussing possible topics for a political debate in one of his Spanish classes, a student shouted out, "Señor, what do you think about gay marriage?" He shot back, "Why, are you proposing?"

Bob was a beloved B Form (5th grade) teacher. An avid bird-watcher, every year he took interested boys on the White House Bird Count. As he got older, he would floss his teeth while listening to the boys give speeches and then fall asleep with his stocking feet on the desk. He said, "I knew it was time to retire when I went to the drinking fountain to sharpen my pencil."

Frank would zing erasers at boys who gave a wrong answer. He would probably be arrested for that today.

One morning, two women on the maintenance staff got in a fist fight in their changing room because both were in a relationship with the same man, also on the maintenance staff.

Bryan Leithauser was using the faculty kitchen to roast some broccoli that was going to be a part of a meal for a homeless ministry. The strong smell of cooking broccoli filled the halls (the faculty kitchen was not properly ventilated) and caused the students to run out of their classes gagging.

Sally, the Upper School administrative assistant, would not answer the phone in the morning until she finished the *New York Times* crossword puzzle. She also kept a bottle of gin in the bottom draw of her desk for years. It had been a leftover from a school event. She swore she never used it.

The Lower School music teacher also kept a bottle of whiskey in the upright piano. He did use it.

An English teacher struck fear into the hearts of her students by her brilliant and exacting standards. Frank Fitts IV recalled he once thought he had written a really good paper. When it was returned, he could barely read it for the comments in red ink, which ended abruptly halfway through. At the end it said "See Me!" When he went to see her, she told him she stopped grading his paper because she was afraid her red pen would run out of ink.

This teacher had been given a gift of a Weber grill, and for years it remained behind the door of the office she shared with Bryan Leithauser until the renovation of the new wing. The boys never asked why it was there.

Bob Andreoli is a very popular math teacher and Dean of Students. Boring math class? He'd challenge religion class to a game of "tennis baseball." Philo with Billow would jump at the chance. Bob was also the wrestling coach. You could wrestle him in the hallway for extra credit on math tests.

Rob Shurmer, Suzanne Woods, and I once got busted by Headmaster Wilson for creating a sign that did not meet with his approval. The newly completed Marriott Hall, a very contemporary stone, steel, and glass building, bumped up against the Lane Johnson Building, a Gothic stone structure. The always-clever Rob Shurmer printed a sign as you entered the new building that read "You are now entering East Berlin." We taped it on the wall outside his office. Just as we did so, the headmaster walked by. When he saw the three of us in Shurmer's office, he poked his head in the door. All he said was, "Take it down." We realized later it could also be viewed on Rob's computer screen.

Sherry Rusher, Linda DeBord, and Paul Herman were interviewing candidate for a job. Paul asked her what she liked to do in her spare time. She replied, "Have great sex." She did *not* get the job.

Paul started writing with his left hand because he heard it would help him fight off dementia. The only problem was the students couldn't read his writing on the board.

The head of the kitchen was often searching for greenery at the very last minute for table centerpieces. He would run outside the school, hide in the bushes, and yank branches off trees, which is absolutely forbidden by the All Hallows Guild, which oversees the care of the gardens and landscaping of the Cathedral Close. Running back inside, he would say, "Don't tell Mrs. Steuart!" Peggy Steuart, president of the All Hallows Guild, was often seated at the head table—which always had the most beautiful of his arrangements.

Pete Gordon was for many years head of the Lower School and was known for his common sense. A former marine, he had many expressions for which he is remembered. My favorite is "You can't blow sh*t out of a trumpet, boys!" (I still don't know what that means.)

Upon learning about the mandatory sexual harassment sensitivity training day with the National Cathedral School, Mary Hardman quipped, "Sexual harassment! Quick! Where's my lipstick?!"

Knowing how much I tried to avoid curriculum committee meetings, the committee chair, Sherry Rusher, would regularly ask me on the way to the meeting, "Are you going to have another pastoral crisis this afternoon?"

In response to glowing praise for our religion program from a visitor, Brooks Hundley, the Upper School chaplain, said to me, "If they only knew the real story."

Facilities manager Bob Oldham, sometimes frustrated by the wear and tear on the building, could be heard saying, "This would be a great school if it weren't for these damn kids!"

Joyce Murphy, administrative assistant for the Lower School, never missed a day of work and was always "at her post" way before the start of the school day. The only time she was running late and hurrying to her desk, Joyce heard Bob Oldham, with his touch of a southern accent, call out, "The b*tch is in!" Joyce was horrified, thinking he was referring to her as a b*tch! Bob was actually exclaiming that the new bench for outside the Lower School had been delivered.

One year when it seemed a number of our students were not getting into the college of their choice, one of the mothers (a social worker) started a support group for "mothers of deferred students."

A Lower School teacher saw a pill on a secretary's desk. Assuming it was an aspirin, he said, "I need this," and swallowed it. It was a birth control pill.

Students and teachers all eat lunch together in the refectory. Lunch begins with grace and ends with announcements. One day, the computer teacher—a brave woman working at an all-boys school—got up and announced, "Quit coming to me with your three-and-a-half-inch floppies."

I Just Love Working at... Sidwell?

In our early years as younger faculty, we would often gather at Cactus Cantina on Wisconsin Avenue for happy hour. As the evening wore on things might get a little loud. One particular evening we were making quite a commotion and were wearing hats made out of our table napkins. Realizing that we were being observed by many patrons as we were leaving the restaurant, lower school teacher and LaCrosse coach John Nostrant yelled out. "I just love working at Sidwell!"

Sidwell Friends School is a Quaker school a mile down Wisconsin Avenue from St Albans.

THE LOOK

The Reverend Daniel Heischman was the head of the Upper School. More than any other person I know, Dan has perfected the art of *the look*. Ask any student or faculty member that has known Dan—they'll know what I'm talking about. If any situation came up the details of which Dan might question or disapprove, you got *the look*.

One faculty work day, we had all gathered in Trapier Theater to listen to a guest speaker. It was unbelievably boring. Bryan Leithauser passed me a note, which made me start laughing. I couldn't stop. I was so embarrassed, I crawled on the floor pretending to look for a pencil. Once I came up, Dan, who was in front of us, shot us *the look*.

It only got worse when Bryan mouthed the words, "What's with Dan?" Back down to the floor I went.

Later, Ann Selinger and I were in my office and Dan walked in. We asked him how he learned to give *the look*. He said, "What look?"

The look is extremely effective because more than just about any other school administrator I have known, Dan is respected and loved by students, parents, and faculty alike. Luckily, he also has a hilarious sense of humor, because I once almost gave him a heart attack.

One night we were addressing the VI Form parents. Dan followed me and gave a perceptive and eloquent summation of the year, as was his custom.

When he sat down, I said, "That was terrific."

Dan: "Thanks."

Me: "I just can't believe that last thing you said."

Dan: "What did I say?"

Me: "And in conclusion, they're just f-ing great kids."

Dan: "I said *what?*"

Me: I'm *kidding!*

That time *the look* was one of total panic.

THE RED REVERENDS

When I became the senior chaplain, we had the extreme fortune of hiring the Reverend Claudia Gould Tielking to be chaplain to the Lower School. I thought it important for the boys to have a woman priest in that role. Both Claudia and I have red hair, and the boys dubbed us "The Red Reverends."

One unexpected thing that happened was that a boy would from time to time develop a crush on Claudia. A mother laughingly reported that her son came home from school one day and remarked to her that her legs did not appear "as smooth as Reverend Gould's." Luckily, she had a great sense of humor.

In one amazing meeting with a mother who was having an issue disciplining her son, she asked Claudia if she would handle it because, the mother said, "I'm more his friend."

Claudia immediately replied, "No, you're his mother."

In another encounter a mother came to listen to her son read a lesson in chapel. Claudia, pleased that she had come, welcomed her, and the mother said, "I came to see what this sh*t was all about." Claudia later thought she should have replied, "Thank you, I have devoted my life to this sh*t!"

While at St. Albans, Claudia was biking on the George Washington Parkway and was seriously injured after being hit by a car. In what was a totally characteristic thing for her to do because of her devotion to her job, when I got to the emergency room she took off her oxygen mask and gasped, "I don't think I'll be able to make it to work Monday!"

As it turned out, her recuperation from her injuries took months.

From time to time both Claudia and I would together attend chaplains' conferences and were amazed at how many attendees were unhappy in their jobs and felt a lack of support from their heads of school. Fortunately, that was never the case with either of us while at St. Albans, and we would always return totally grateful for the support we had.

Claudia, now retired, became the mother of two and married literally a rocket scientist, which the boys thought was totally awesome.

A Fifty-Yard Pass Completion

Many years ago, a dispute arose over the dismissal of the headmaster. It rocked the St. Albans community to its core. What I want to write about are not the details of the arguments one way or another, but the bonding that took place among my colleagues that we will remember for the rest of our lives.

As the Governing Board met in the cathedral's south tower, members of the faculty, staff, alumni, and friends gathered below in the nave in support of the headmaster. It turned out to be a *very* long evening.

For many of us, children of the '60s, now in our khakis, docksiders, tweed jackets, sweater sets, and pearls, it brought back memories of standing up for what we believed was important.

Many of us brought papers to grade and books to read, but some of the younger faculty had other ideas. To the delight of those of us who watched, wheelchair races commenced up and down the nave, which incidentally is so long, one could lay the Washington Monument on its side. When after practice the coaches arrived, a football appeared, and well after midnight we witnessed probably the longest pass ever thrown in the cathedral.

The next morning as I walked bleary-eyed into the Burling faculty lounge, there were my beloved colleagues sound asleep on chairs and couches, determined to meet their classes and waking one another when it was time.

Though the events of those weeks were difficult, no one can ever take away the sense of community among the faculty and the memory of what I believe was a fifty-yard pass completion.

THE GIFT

A man once appeared in the doorway of Pam Grant, the headmaster's secretary. She knew him to be a St. Albans father and grandfather. He pulled an envelope out of his pocket and handed it to her. It was addressed to the headmaster, and Pam said she would see that it got to him. The envelope held a check addressed to the school for one million dollars.

GENTLEMAN JACK

Jack "Gentleman Jack" McCune was for years the head of the Upper School and then became headmaster. Jack earned his nickname by encouraging civility and respect and was as kind a person as I have ever known . . . so kind that he had difficulty delivering bad news, whether it had to do with student discipline or confronting a faculty or staff member with some sort of grievance.

One year after the Honor Council had unanimously agreed on the expulsion of a student, the student walked out of a meeting with Jack with a smile and a thumbs-up. He was back the next year.

Another year, as the school was assessing its curricular changes, it became apparent we didn't have enough sign-ups for the Japanese elective. Sweet and kind, the Japanese teacher was a tiny woman who had some difficulty understanding English (for example, we gently had to explain to her the difference between the men's and ladies' rooms), and it fell to Jack to deliver the news that unfortunately there would not be a spot for her on the faculty in the next school year. At the end of the school year, we had a lovely farewell and thank-you for her service to the school.

As one might expect, Jack handled the situation with great care. So great, in fact, that the next year at the opening faculty meetings, there she was! Always one to care for everyone, he arranged for her to stay on until she could find work. My last memory of her is on the kitchen staff.

The angriest I ever saw Jack was while dealing with a very difficult faculty member, and while most of us in frustration might have delivered a different expletive, the worst I ever heard from Jack was "Nuts!"

Jack left us far too early, and at his funeral I quoted Fred Buechner's definition of "saint" in his book *Wishful Thinking*: "In his holy flirtation with the world, God drops an occasional handkerchief. These handkerchiefs are called saints."

THE SNAKE AND THE SHRINK

I do not consider myself a therapist at all but after my own positive experience in therapy combined with my religious journey, I wanted to create in my classes a similar "safe" place where students could make their vulnerabilities known and not feel judged. From time to time they would reveal their hesitancy or their own experiences with psychiatrists or psychologists, both good and bad.

We had a consulting psychologist associated with the school who had the good sense to have his office and hours off campus because of the embarrassment that often accompanies realizing the need for help. I would also show the movie *Ordinary People*, an extraordinary film that chronicles a young man's journey of self-discovery while in therapy following the death of his brother. The following is an example of a situation with one of my more-reluctant students.

I had a monthly consultation with the head of adolescent medicine at the Psychiatric Institute of Washington. They were extraordinarily helpful meetings. I would bring situations that would present themselves, and he would try to help me figure out how best to help the kids and parents seeking guidance.

One year we had boy who was having serious anger-management issues, and his parents were desperately trying to get him to see a counselor. He would meet with me, but wouldn't see a psychiatrist or psychologist because in his eyes they were for "crazy" people. After a number of sessions with me, wherein I could describe my own successful experience in therapy, he very reluctantly agreed to go see Dr Brain because he was a friend of mine.

I offered to drive him to the psychiatrist's office in nearby Bethesda. After we arrived, I sat down on a bench outside the building while he went in to meet with the psychiatrist. While I was sitting there reading, a young man came and sat down beside me. He said, "Hi! You like snakes?"

He then proceeded to pull a snake out of his jacket. Pointing to the doctor's office and smiling, he said, "They don't like snakes in there."

Startled, I explained that I didn't mind snakes so much, except for when they surprised me in the yard (or in someone's jacket), but I was really thinking, "Oh no! I hope he leaves before my student comes out or he'll never come back!"

Luckily he left.

The boy came out of the office several minutes later and went on to have very successful treatment and a great relationship with his therapist.

I have yet to tell him about the young man with the snake.

A COMPASSIONATE INSTITUTION

I feel fortunate in my time as chaplain of St. Albans to have worked for three great headmasters. Each saw the Little Sanctuary as the heart of the school. It is where the St. Albans community gathers twice a week to speak about what matters most in their lives, and is where the faculty, staff, and students begin and end their school year. It is also the place where many choose to celebrate the beginning and the end of a life.

Each man held the pastoral care of the community as his top priority. When someone needed help, it often required the financial resources of the school as well as the legal and professional support of our alumni and faculty.

St. Albans has a mandatory social service component, with the boys required to perform a specific number of hours before they enter their senior year. Many go well beyond their required hours. Living in the city, students, faculty, and staff are confronted daily with the issues homeless and mentally ill people face. It is particularly hard when that person is one of your own.

One day one of the kids came into my office and said, "Um, Mr. Billow, there's a guy in a robe and bare feet walking around the Little Sanctuary."

I had a hunch who it was. A brilliant scholar/athlete while attending STA, he began exhibiting signs of schizophrenia while in college. He has had several name changes. From time to time he returns to the Close when he goes off his meds—I think because he felt safe and welcome there. He is certainly welcome, *if* he stays on his meds, which he knows.

I got him into my office and again explained to him that he couldn't be at St. Albans unless he was on his meds. I asked if he wanted me to take him to the hospital to get back on them. He emphatically said, "Yes!" So I sent word to my next class that I wouldn't be there (never disappointing to the students), and off we went to the ER at Georgetown University Hospital.

When we arrived, having recognized both of us, the nurses ushered us into a room. As the afternoon wore on, we were joined by a doctor, a nurse, and a social worker, who tried to determine whether he needed hospitalization while waiting for his meds to work.

In the middle of the interview, my former student said in a loud voice, "Wait a minute! Wait a minute! I have a question for Reverend Billow!"

I said, "OK."

He asked, "Do you remember the *first* time you had sex with a woman?"

Everyone was a bit taken aback. Although it was a somewhat personal question, and as I was single and I was wearing my clergy collar, I hesitated and then simply answered honestly, "Yes."

He said, "That's what I'm talking about!"

THE GREEN COAT

I walked to work at St. Albans every day from my house on 38th Street, which was just a couple of blocks away. There was a homeless man named

Carl who often stood on the corner of Wisconsin and Massachusetts Avenues, and we would often speak. Everybody knew him.

One morning after Christmas break, I was on my way to school. Carl stopped me and told me he needed an overcoat. As I had many in my closet, I said, "Sure, I can get you a coat." I do not know what prompted me to say it, but I then asked, "What color would you like?" He said, "Green."

My heart sank. I had one green coat, a very expensive Polo overcoat I had just gotten for Christmas from my sister and brother-in-law, Kim and Larry. I thought to myself, "OK, Will, this is a test of who you are as a human being." I said, "I have a nice green coat," and I went home to get it. When I brought it back to him, he clearly loved it. He put it right on.

I preached about it in chapel to the kids. The lesson was Jesus saying, "Where your treasure is, there will your heart be also." I wasn't patting myself on the back—I had learned an important lesson about treasuring "things." The kids loved the chapel. For weeks they would tell me they spotted Carl in my coat.

All that winter, I would greet him on the corner wearing the coat. The problem was, I wondered if I should say anything to Kim and Larry. I was sure Kim had spent a lot of money on the gift.

During a phone conversation with Larry, he asked me, "How do you like the coat?" I said, "A lot!" Then, not wanting to lie and because I had gotten such a great response from the kids, I told him what I had done and said, "I was hesitant to tell Kim." In a very loud voice he said, "What do you mean Kim?! I bought it!"

Larry still can't believe I did it.

On Being a Mentor

While at St. Columba's and St. Albans, I had the privilege of being a supervisor and mentor to folks who are some of the finest clergy I know.

All of them will laughingly tell you that when it came time for their evaluations, I did it in a rather unconventional way, an idea I "stole" from my colleague Bob Andreoli. He evaluated his math students by having them write their own evaluation in the third person and then would tell them whether or not he concurred. Such an exercise would tell me much about their self-awareness, which is an attribute very important to have, particularly for clergy. If they're not self-aware, you've got trouble.

SPORTS: THE LAX REV

I once agreed to drive one of the vans up to New York for a game between the STA lacrosse team and a public high school team outside of Syracuse. I honestly can't remember if we won or lost, but it's what happened on the way home that I remember most vividly.

We were on the Garden State Parkway without benefit of E-ZPass, which meant we had to stop and pay several tolls along the way. At one particular stop, I thought the guy in the ticket booth was waving me through before I paid the toll (should have known better, as it is Jersey). Anyways, he yelled, "Stop!" I slammed on the brakes and it jerked all the kids forward, either waking them up or sending the homework they were doing onto the floor of the van.

The STA LAX team PHOTO COURTESY OF ST. ALBANS SCHOOL

The ticket booth guy yelled, "What in the hell are you doing?" I yelled back an apology and said, "I thought you were waving me through." He yelled back, "What would I do that for?"

A response came from the back of the van that I was not expecting: "Hey buddy! Don't f**k with our reverend!" The ticket booth guy looked at me wide-eyed, and all I could do was put my head on the steering wheel. With that, I paid the toll.

The guy then said, "Just get out of here!" As I pulled away, I looked in the rearview mirror and every single kid was "flipping him off."

Luckily the rented van I was driving had no way of identifying us as being from STA. That championship year the team presented me with an inscribed beer mug. It reads "The LAX Rev."

HOLY SH*T!

One of my favorite things to do was to go to football camp with the team in the late summer before school begins. I confess I was very relieved the coach found a place in the mountains of the Shenandoah Valley, because the heat and humidity in DC in the late summer can be brutal.

David is one of my best friends. He was a senior my first year, and *thank God* I never had to teach him.

Dave played football while at North Carolina and for a time was on the staff of Notre Dame, working under Lou Holtz, until he came to us as a teacher/coach while he attended law school. At one point he considered seminary, but when he told me, I literally spit out the margarita I was drinking and that was the end of that.

One year during football camp at Camp Paddy Run in West Virginia, I walked out to the ball field to watch practice as Dave was berating the defensive line. He yelled, "You all look like sh*t!" One of the boys whispered to him, "Coach Mohler, Reverend Billow is right behind you." Dave turned around, looked at me, and said, "Oh, excuse me, Reverend . . . *holy* sh*t!"

SIN IS FUN!

Sin is something the Bible explains we are *not* to do, but once a year I attend a weekend with Washington friends in Rehoboth Beach, Delaware, where lying, cheating, and stealing is allowed on Easter weekend!

The "missionaries" PHOTO COURTESY OF JOYCE MURPHY

It happens within the context of a scavenger hunt on Holy Saturday, traditionally the day between Jesus's death and resurrection, when we remember his spirit was absent from the earth, but I'm not sure the particular significance of that has ever occurred to any of us who participate. You can say or do anything to win—throw people off course, even steal from another team. The only things you cannot do? You can*not* shoplift, and you can*not* go over the speed limit.

The hunt is organized by C. A. and Joe Knoll, St. Albans parents. Joe is a Washington lawyer; C. A. is a decorator. C. A.'s father, Dr. Francis Fabrizio, was on the faculty at Georgetown University and for a time owned the Henlopen Hotel in Rehoboth Beach.

The game includes many of my friends from Washington who for years have vacationed together at the beach. Over the years the couples have included Jan and Pat O'Donnell, Damien and Maggie DuFour, Doug and Holly Davidson, Mike and Ann McInerny, and Joyce and Bill Murphy. All except for Ann are good Catholics. She's Episcopalian. They graciously invite a few Protestants to participate, including Peter and Connie Collis, Marcia Eisinger, John and Peggy Powell, B. A. and Corky Crovato, and me. All of the grown children are invited to participate as well. The women have a social group that meets regularly called "the missionaries," although the title has nothing to do with evangelism.

We are all given a series of clues and drive through the town of Rehoboth Beach searching for envelopes the Knolls leave with various shopkeepers who are all "in" on the hunt. So are the police. We are required to buy things on our list—that's probably why the merchants allow it to happen. One year I commandeered a bread truck for a ride by bribing the driver with a six-pack of beer.

The weekend always ends with an Easter morning Eucharist with all the families attending. Afterward some folks go on to Catholic Mass, because after such a weekend they might question the legitimacy of my priesthood. I can understand that for any number of reasons.

The only other time I remember participating in something similar was at the pancake race at Washington National Cathedral. I wasn't aware of any particular "rules," so while we were racing I threw a banana peel in front of Elizabeth Orens, the chaplain of the National Cathedral

School. The moment was captured by a photographer and ended up in the *Washington Post* and *USA Today*.

I was disqualified.

I remember while in seminary Professor Richard Reid posed the question, "Why do people sin?" All the seminarians thought up profound answers to this deep existential question until he again asked, "Why do people sin?" and then answered his own question: "Sin is fun!"

GRANDPARENTS DAY

One of my favorite days all year was Grandparents Day. It generally started out with chapel. Grandparents have a tendency to get to school *very* early, so beforehand we'd have to race around and find boys and match them up with their grandparents. Once that was done, we could begin.

We'd make sure we'd sing all the old favorites, including "A Mighty Fortress" and "Holy, Holy, Holy." The boys would read the lessons; the headmaster would speak. After prayers, off the grandparents would go to classes with their grandsons and then the real fun would begin.

One year in the Lower School, one of the teachers asked his students to tell him something special about their grandparent. Several of the boys said what you might expect: "My grandmother is a good cook." "My grandfather taught me how to fish." But one of the boys raised his hand and when called on he said enthusiastically, "My grandmother has been married *three* times!" His grandmother quickly responded, "I've been *widowed* each time!"

One of my favorite stories to which I was a witness was when I attended a Grandparents Day at Summit School in Winston-Salem, North Carolina, with my dear friend Ann Willis, a grandmother who, after she sneaked a cigarette between classes out in the sandbox, had to go into drama class.

The teacher welcomed all of us and then asked us to put on our pretend "magic glasses." Ann wasn't having any of it until the teacher shamed her into it by saying, "I see we don't all have our magic glasses on." As Ann's reluctant fingers circled her eyes, the teacher then said, "Do you all see the oogly, oogly monster?"

Ann loudly responded, "I have trouble enough seeing what I know is there!"

The Greatest Generation

It's a great life if you don't weaken.

—Mary Davidson Bryan

I have always loved the old-timers. They have seen the school through *everything*: fundraising, scandal, board divisions, firings, curriculum changes, education, number of times chapel meets a week (we're going for quality, not quantity), and the biggest thing of all—the snow cancellation policy!

The story was, STA *never* closed. From the kids' (and faculty's) perspective, there was nothing worse than to hear on the TV or radio, "DC public schools are closed . . .," eliciting moans in the classrooms and the hallways as the kids toiled away at their desks. Finally, the mayor of DC pleaded with the headmaster, for the sake of the safety of the students and faculty, to change the snow policy. Now the three school heads confer to make the call.

I recently officiated at a memorial for Maurice Heartfield—one of STA's most ardent supporters—in the Little Sanctuary. At eighty-eight, he remained as sharp as a tack until his COPD took him from us. As we gathered for his funeral, I was never so glad that in a recent renovation we made the chapel handicap accessible. I have never seen so many wheelchairs, walkers, and canes.

As I entered the chapel for a pre-funeral check, Tom Brokaw's "greatest generation" greeted me with, "For Pete's sake, Will, when are you going to do something about these damn hard pews!" "Will! You have a leak over in the corner!" "Will! Turn up the lights! I can't see a thing!"

I began the service with a greeting, welcoming them all. Quoting them, I pointed to headmaster Vance Wilson and said, "As to your suggestions, there's your man!" and I reminded them, "Maurice wouldn't have had his memorial anywhere else." And, of course, neither will they.

After the service, one widow quipped, "Couldn't hear a thing . . ."

SCHOOL AS PARISH

One of the things that struck me after a number of years at St. Albans was that the school began to function as a parish. We were Episcopal in name and liturgy but with a religiously diverse community of families. Muslim, Jew, Hindu, Christian, Buddhist, Baha'i, and those with no faith—it didn't seem to matter. All were welcome under the STA umbrella. In an interesting twist, one year Hazem Abu Ghazeleh, a Muslim, was elected senior warden of the student vestry by popular vote. He saw it as his responsibility to maintain the Christian traditions of STA.

We saw Jesus's message as one of inclusion, not exclusion, and in so doing we never had to be afraid to mention his name. We never proselytized. We just tried to be true to his message, and it worked to create a loving interfaith community. To this day the school remains a spiritual home to many and sees a number of weddings, funerals, and baptisms of students, faculty, staff, alumni, and their families.

When I arrived at St. Albans, true to its reputation, I encountered a bunch of really smart people—students and faculty alike. However, several department heads seemed to operate in their own fiefdoms and were not at all collegial. Competition and sarcasm seemed to rule the day in the early years I was there. Unfortunately, the kids picked up on this.

LOSSES AND OTHER TRAGEDIES

Over the years I think what really changed the culture of the school was a series of losses with which we were faced personally and societally. They involved the deaths of a fourth-grader, several faculty members, school parents, and alumni, two of whom were murdered in separate incidents within a year's time, in addition to a horrific lightning strike in the middle of a lacrosse game and the death of the Bishop of Washington. We also faced terror threats, which undermined our sense of security and well-being.

After Jesus's death, the scripture tells us the Apostles gathered and "their eyes were opened." In a similar way, as students and faculty gathered in the chapel after each incident, our eyes were opened to one another. So were our hearts. Here are some of the stories.

Billy, 1988

Billy Kroener was a fun-loving and popular member of the St. Albans class of 1986. He and three other students were killed by a drunk driver in their second year of college in Ohio. The tragedy of their deaths was heightened by the trial of the young woman who hit them. And St. Albans was deeply affected by the death of a beloved classmate—and was taught an enormous lesson about the dangers of drunk driving.

Bishop John T. Walker, 1989

When Bishop John T. Walker died, I think I felt something akin to what the disciples felt when they lost Jesus.

One of the first African-American bishops of the Episcopal Church, John Thomas Walker was born in Barnesville, Georgia, and grew up in Detroit. During the days of segregation, he was the first African American admitted to Virginia Theological Seminary in Alexandria, Virginia. While with some of his white fellow seminarians, he was refused service at restaurants in Alexandria and DC. It was the first time many of them had seen such a thing firsthand.

Gentle and kind, John harbored no resentment. Love was the guiding force of his life, and as a result he was able to break down barriers, both racial and political, which served him well throughout his ministry but particularly in Washington, still a deeply prejudiced southern town. Only one restaurant in DC would serve him, Old Europe on Wisconsin Avenue in Georgetown.

After he was ordained, while on a trip to Costa Rica, he met Maria, his wife of twenty-seven years. Together they raised three children, now grown: Tommy, a filmmaker in New York City; Ana, a pediatrician in Washington, DC; and Carli, a urologist in New Haven, Connecticut. I am honored that Ana's son John is my godson.

After serving in a Detroit parish, John became chaplain at St. Paul's School in Concord, New Hampshire. From there he came to Washington National Cathedral, where he served as a canon under cathedral dean Francis Sayre. John became dean after Sayre's retirement. He became Bishop Suffragen in 1971, was elected Bishop Coadjutor in 1976, and became Bishop of Washington in 1977.

The Right Reverend John T. Walker, Bishop of Washington
PHOTO COURTESY OF ST. ALBANS SCHOOL

As anyone who comes to Washington will see, one building alone soars high above all the others. The National Cathedral sits atop Mount St. Alban, one of the highest points in Washington. The building is important, but only important as long as those who serve within it do so with humility and grace.

In his various roles while in Washington, John was a guiding force in the civil rights and Vietnam antiwar movements, advising senators and presidents. He was present the day Dr. Martin Luther King Jr. delivered his last Sunday sermon at the National Cathedral, shortly before his assassination in Memphis. John's wife, Maria, attended the service that day and recalled "how tired" Dr. King seemed. Even so, she said he preached for forty-five minutes. Dean Sayre and John realized how important it was to give over the pulpit to Dr. King that day.

John found special joy in children. He loved the Cathedral Schools. Even while bishop, he preached regularly in chapel at Beauvoir, the National Cathedral elementary school. I spent a lot of time with him as I began my chaplaincy at St. Albans. He once told me that when he retired he wanted to go back to being a school chaplain. He also said he wanted to learn to play the piano.

On a humorous note, not long before he died, I accompanied John to a reception at the home of Charlie and Betty Price at Virginia Seminary. It was the same week he had been arrested demonstrating against apartheid outside the South African Embassy. I was the designated driver. When John ordered his cocktail, Annilee Brown, the hostess of the seminary, looked at John and quipped, "If you're driving, you better be careful. You've already been arrested once this week!"

As fate would have it, John died unexpectedly of complications from heart surgery on September 30, 1989. This was a day after the anniversary of the laying of the cathedral cornerstone, which took place on September 29, 1907, with President Theodore Roosevelt in attendance. The cathedral was dedicated a year after John's death on September, 29, 1990, with President and Mrs. George H. W. Bush attending.

Just as people look for "something" to believe in, like God, I think they look for "someone" to believe in as well. I think John was that "someone" for me, and not just for me but for the people he encountered in his life. And not only did we believe in him, he believed in us.

As anyone who knew him will tell you, to be in his presence was to be in what the author and theologian Marcus Borg would call being in the presence of a "spirit person," one for whom God is an "experiential reality." You just feel something special being around these people.

As Bishop James Montgomery advised me as a seminarian so many years ago, it is important to *know* God, not just *know about* God, and I finally met someone who did.

It was John.

Wisdom of Desmond Tutu

I first met Desmond Tutu at John and Maria Walker's house the evening before John's funeral, which was held in October of 1989. John and Desmond were close friends. After knowing John, my life was forever changed. I think that is because he really believed in me . . . and when you experience that from someone in life, particularly in a career, it inspires confidence and your life is never the same. You begin to believe in yourself. Perhaps that's why the disciples felt the way they did about Jesus.

Like John, Desmond Tutu inspires that sort of belief and confidence in everyone he encounters. He was interviewed in *Life* magazine years ago about God's solidarity with us. Desmond referred to a story told of a Jew in a concentration camp being made to clean out toilets. He was being taunted by his Nazi guard, who said, "Where is your God now, Jew?" The man quietly replied, "He is right here with me, in the muck."

Adrien, 1989

Adrien Lescaze, a C-Former, was killed as a result of injuries he suffered in a car accident. He and his sister, a student at the National Cathedral School, were broadsided by a car while on their way to school. What I remember most vividly is that for several days, the hallways outside the ICU at Children's Hospital were lined with students from NCS and STA. The day Adrien died, we learned his organs would give life to another child, and the next day we read of a successful heart transplant at the hospital. It was the first heart transplant ever performed at Children's National Medical Center in Washington.

His service was held in the cathedral, and the one special request his classmates made was to sing his favorite song, "Joy to the World," which was met by some resistance by the music department at the cathedral until the bishop intervened.

Bishop Walker asked Adrien's parents if they might wish for his ashes to be interred in the cathedral. They declined, thinking his ashes might better be buried in an open space because he was a little boy who loved to run and play. Together we found the perfect place on the Cathedral Close known for lots of games of hide-and-seek and tag. Unfortunately, the Cathedral Foundation rules do not allow for such a burial. So, when

I asked the bishop for permission, he said, "If you do it, I don't want to know about it," and winked at me.

Vaughn, 1990

When Vaughn Keith, a classics teacher at St. Albans, was dying of AIDS, what I remember best is the compassion of the students as they saw his condition deteriorate. Their concern was not whether or not they might catch this dreadful disease, but whether or not they should come to class if they had a cold, fearing Vaughn might get it with his compromised immune system. I credit our science department for keeping us well informed about the nature of the disease, because at the time it was greatly misunderstood. Headmaster Mark Mullin dealt with the situation with enormous compassion.

Tiger, 1991

Tiger Ferris, one of our coaches, was living in a makeshift apartment in the athletic building when he died of lung disease. He was a tennis coach. He and the Lower School chaplain, the Reverend Jamie Evans, known as Rev Ev, operated a car repair business for parents, faculty, and students under the archway that connected the Lower and Upper Schools. Pam Grant, assistant to Pete Gordon, the head of the Lower School, would receive and sign for the auto parts delivered to her door.

Billey, 1991

Henri Billey, known simply as "Billey," was chair of the language department, taught French, and was the Dean of Students. He had a stick for a pointer named "Maxime" and would wield it around the classroom, threatening to strike the boys with it if they got the wrong answer. I never heard he ever actually made contact with a student, but he once threw Maxime so hard she stuck in the blackboard. The kids never forgot that.

The Lightning Strike, May 17, 1991

When I switched on the computer on May 17, 2016, I found a subject in my inbox that read "25 years ago." The first sentence of the email said: "This note is significantly overdue (and I mean significantly) but given that 25 years ago you saved my life, I felt compelled to finally put it together."

Twenty-five years earlier, the sender of the email, Jeff Cohen, was a junior at Landon School and had come to watch the Landon Bears take on the St. Albans Bulldogs in lacrosse. It began as a beautiful spring day with a crystal blue sky, but as all who live in DC know, as the heat in the afternoon rises, the threat of serious thunderstorms increases, as was the case on that fateful day.

It was a day full of celebrations. It began with Queen Elizabeth II making an appearance at the National Cathedral, which sits at the center of the Cathedral Close surrounded by its three schools: St. Albans, the National Cathedral School for Girls, and Beauvoir. There were picnics in the Bishop's Garden, and the schools were in joyful expectation of their prize days and graduation ceremonies, which were only a few weeks away.

But the STA LAX team and its supporters didn't care about all that. This was *our* year and the championship was on the line, and we were playing Landon!

There was a rally before the game. Boys of all ages had painted their faces blue and white and headed down to the field to the beat of the drum. They were joined by parents, alums, faculty, and staff of STA and surrounding schools, as this was the biggest game of the year.

As the game commenced, our athletic director, Skip Grant, was keeping a watchful eye on the sky. The sky was still blue above our heads, but black clouds were quickly making their way toward us. When he received word of lightning, he immediately called the game and everyone ran for shelter. But it was too late.

As the rain began, I huddled in the snack shack next to the field. Immediately, we saw a flash of lightning and a crack of thunder as loud as I have ever heard, and then just . . . silence. Then, a voice called, "Help!"

I ran to where the voice came from, and at the top of the steps that led to the tennis pavilion, I looked down and saw bodies lying in a fan shape surrounding an enormous tree.

I didn't know what to do, so I did what I had been taught years before. I ran to the first body I came to—a boy. I checked to see if he was breathing. He wasn't. So I started CPR.

The boy, Jeff Cohen, started to breathe.

When the paramedics arrived and got to Jeff and me, I gratefully put him in their hands. I looked around and remember vividly Tom Carroll, my good friend and colleague, administering CPR right next to me.

The rest of the afternoon is really a blur to me. Twelve people had been hit by lightning. I now understand that a lightning bolt had hit the tree and everyone standing on the roots was blown off their feet, which explains the fan shape.

I rode in an ambulance to Suburban Hospital with one of my students and remember feeling it was important to get to every hospital to check on those who had been injured. Then I heard there had been a death, so I headed to Georgetown Hospital. I can't remember how I got there.

Kind nurses ushered me into a room. I remember it was cold and the light in the room had a bluish tint to it. There was a stainless steel table, and on that table wrapped in sheets was a boy with red hair. I remember feeling horribly guilty because I didn't recognize him. I said out loud to him, "Who are you? Who are you?" and then I did the only thing I could. I said a prayer and waited with him until I heard his parents had arrived.

The boy was Noah Eig. He was a freshman at Landon, and the boy on whom Tom Carroll had been administering CPR. Noah had been leaning against the tree.

Upon reflection, what has been very important for me to realize is that the biblical experience of "the Holy" can be a beautiful thing or a terrifying thing. That day I experienced both.

Jeff is now happily married, living in New York City, and the father of two children.

Monty, 1992

R. Montgomery Raiser, St. Albans class of 1988, was known as "Monty." He, along with his father, Victor, and three others, was killed in a plane crash in Alaska shortly after his graduation from Princeton. His mother, Molly, taught for a time in the lower school. The service for father and son was held in the National Cathedral with both the Clintons and the Gores attending. Vic was a national financial cochair of the Clinton-Gore campaign.

Monty was an enormously gifted student-athlete with a wonderful sense of humor. We rarely saw him without a camera around his neck. He would frequently stop in my office and ask, "So, Will, what's shakin'?" I have always imagined he might have become a photojournalist. He always called me by my first name, which always struck me as funny. We all marveled at the strength of Molly and her daughter, Skye, as they dealt with the enormity of their loss. They, and we, cherish our memories of Monty and Vic.

Donald, 1992

Donald Brown, the school scheduler and chair of the math department, was a diabetic who refused to obey doctor's orders. He had rather exacting standards, such as "Boards," which involved making the one poor boy who displeased him wash the blackboards with a sponge to his specifications. He would also make boys pick up his laundry at the dry cleaners. He had a sign in his office above the clock that said, "Time passes . . . will you?"

No faculty member had the nerve to cross him, or he would schedule your classes on opposite sides of the Cathedral Close so you would have to run from one class to the next.

He could not abide the faculty member who occupied the classroom next to his and kept the shade on his door permanently pulled so he didn't have to look at him as he entered and exited his classroom.

We once heard another faculty member he disliked whistling the tune "If I Only Had a Brain." Donald shot me a knowing glance.

One of the greatest compliments I ever got in my life was when, after Donald's death, a student, Charles Manger, told me Donald said of me, "Billow—he isn't very bright, but he's a damn good chaplain."

Donald was found dead in his apartment on the top floor of the Lower School building. Unfortunately, his door was directly across the hall from the entrance to the C Form (4th grade) room. Quietly, we informed the C Form teachers, who then kept the children occupied as the paramedics and coroner arrived.

He was a large man, so several of us were enlisted to help carry his body through doorways and down several flights of stairs to the funeral home vehicle. I stood across from one of my colleagues, holding on to his body. With every single step we took down the stairs, my colleague repeated, "It's just a job. It's just a job . . ."

9-11

I remember it being an absolutely beautiful late-summer day in Washington.

We were into the first week of school at St. Albans on September 11, 2001. I was sitting at my desk preparing for class when Ann Selinger appeared in my doorway with an absolutely shocked look on her face and said, "Oh my God! A plane has just flown into the World Trade Center!"

Our first worry was that friends, relatives, and members of the school community might be injured or killed, as many travel to New York City with frequency. A number of our alumni also live there.

Within minutes we heard yet another plane had also flown into the other tower . . . then the Pentagon . . . then Shanksville.

In the midst of our own shock and confusion, we tried our best to keep the children on schedule until, thanks to cell phone use, word started to get out among the student body. Kids were running in and out of my office asking, "Is it true?!" and *panic* started to set in.

As the situation became somewhat clearer, and we understood this to be a terror attack, we decided to assemble the faculty and students in the chapel to gather our thoughts and pray for those who would be affected. As it turned out, that would be all of us.

Our school chapel, the Little Sanctuary, sits atop Mount St. Alban, in the shadow of Washington National Cathedral. It is one of the highest points in the city. While we prayed we heard the sounds of the sirens in the city and of the fighter jets above. After we came out of chapel, we saw the smoke rising from the Pentagon into that clear blue sky.

I remember there being some concern that the cathedral itself might be a target, as it is a massive structure that towers above the city.

The children went back to class until, as a result of the chaos in the city, parents were calling us and their children on their cell phones, wanting to pick them up. The children were told they absolutely could not leave without permission. Teachers abandoned any lesson plans, and many students and teachers gathered in the Trapier Theater to watch the events of the day unfold on the big screen.

I remember not really knowing how concerned to be for our own safety until Karen Hughes, counselor to President George W. Bush, sent word to pick up her child.

Those who live in Washington remember how eerily quiet it was in the skies for the next few hours and days, except for an occasional fighter jet overhead. No planes were allowed to fly.

Several St. Albans families suffered deep personal loss that day.

Casey Knoll, STA '91, who worked in the World Trade Center at Cantor Fitzgerald, was going in late that day. All of his friends from work perished.

Jeremy Glick, the husband of Ann Selinger's daughter's best friend, was on the plane that crashed in Shanksville.

President Bush had been out of the city when the attack occurred and was flown to an undisclosed place of safety. In a chapel talk at St. Albans during the following season of Epiphany, ABC White House correspondent Ann Compton, whose sons attended St. Albans, gave a very moving account of being on Air Force One that day. She said, "When we took off, the clocks on the plane always gave the time you would arrive at your destination—not so on 9-11. We learned the time we would arrive in mid-flight. We weren't flying back to Washington."

Mother and Child Reunion

A young mother with four boys at St. Albans, Katie McGregor, was diagnosed with colon cancer. She was an avid runner in fantastic physical shape. Katie met her diagnosis with sheer grit. Everyone at St. Albans marveled at her determination to come to the boys' events at school "come hell or high water." Her husband, Steve, who has become one of my closest friends, would protest, as he feared for her safety, but there was no stopping her. Steve's job as a senior executive of an oil service company required him to travel a great deal, but he put travel on hold as her illness progressed.

Katie and I met regularly for lunch over the course of her illness. She would choose the restaurants and insisted she pick me up at school until, due to weakness, we'd meet at her home. Katie and Steve had renovated a former embassy, one of the most beautiful homes in the Kalorama section of Washington. The home reflected her exquisite taste in art and architecture, as well as accommodating four growing and very active boys.

One of the things I remember most about Katie was her sense of humor and her curiosity. My own mother had recently died, and she wanted to know how she faced it.

She got a bang out of hearing stories about my mom's bridge club. They were all characters. Mary Spencer was their "designated drunk driver." She would pick each of them up in her enormous Lincoln Town Car and drive them to and from Turnberry Golf Club, in Crystal Lake, Illinois, for bridge. Getting home was always a bit of a challenge, but they felt relatively safe, as there were mostly cornfields between their condos and the club. The bridge club, incidentally, was the source of the funniest jokes I've ever heard.

All the members of the bridge club thought the Hemlock Society was a good idea.

Mom died at seventy-eight of acute respiratory disease. She had called each one of her children separately and told us that if she got a cold or pneumonia, she was thinking she did not want to take any extraordinary measures. She wanted to make sure that was OK with each of us. Of course, it was.

Just as important as how Mom faced her own death, Katie wanted to know how *I* faced my mom's death. Curiously, no one had ever asked me that! So together we went on a journey of discovery.

I have realized my mom still lives in my heart, and because of that, I believe a loving God does not ultimately separate us from the people we love. Katie seemed to take great comfort in that, as her greatest fear was being separated from Steve and her boys.

Katie died on June 25, 2001. She lives on in all of our hearts.

For Willis

Several years later, Katie's death would be followed by that of her youngest son, Willis. The following is the homily I preached at his funeral at Washington National Cathedral in July 2014:

The class of 2007, most of whom came from Beauvoir School, was to be a somewhat challenging one for the faculty and staff of St. Albans School—beginning with what was discovered during their B Form year. As Mary Hardman reminded me, someone had very carefully placed tacks on the toilet seat in the faculty bathroom. When Paul Herman called Willis McGregor into his office about what he had done, Paul said, "Willis, do you realize you could have hurt your teacher?" Willis said, "They weren't meant for Mrs. Hardman! They were meant for . . ." You fill in the blank.

That may have been the first, but certainly not the last, time Katie and Steve McGregor were called into Mr. Herman's office for our dear, sweet, naive, mischievous, often exasperating Willis McGregor.

Those of you who knew him best know that he had what might be described as an "in, but not of, the world" quality about him. He grew up to be a young person often deep in thought, dream, imagination, and wonder. Once when confronted by his parents about a poor math grade, Willis said, and I quote, "Mom, Dad, what difference does it make?*" Some might find that question profound—he was one of those special persons often perplexed by the concrete requirements of the world.*

Oh, and by the way, Steve actually had a cocktail party to celebrate when Willis completed his Lower School Science Fair requirement!

He was a wonderful young man—and I don't use the word wonderful *loosely. His wonderment took him to the many places dreamers go. Sometimes he would take us along—but the truth is he often went alone—but always had loving support, particularly from those who knew him best: Katie, Steve, Nathalie, Andrew, Stephen, Michael, and Gleb.*

In the prelude of the service, we heard Gleb sing Paul Simon's words to "Mother and Child Reunion."

To the McGregor boys I would like to say, armed with that thought—your mother bravely faced her own mortality. She found comfort and courage in the thought that the God who loves us so—as one might understand God as revealed in Jesus—that God would never, ever separate her from the objects of her greatest love—each of you.

So, as it is up to each of us to write our own gospel—in the gospel according to Katie—so be it.

So here's to reunions, and the Willises of this world—the dreamers who delight us and challenge us by asking the question "What difference does it make?"

*Because you see—*they *make the difference.*

Amen.

The Washington Sniper, 2002

In October 2002, Washington, DC, was terrorized by a sniper who was shooting people at random, hiding in the trunk of a car. St. Albans was on lockdown for several days. It was not the easiest time for a school of six hundred boys, most of whom live for sports. Feeling somewhat protected by the privacy of our fields, some sports teams continued to practice outside until the day the *Washington Post* posted a picture of St. Albans boys at play. My assistant, Ann Selinger, observed that despite all the restrictions put on the boys for their safety, she never heard them complain. It exemplified how frightened all of us were at that time.

Tim Russert, 2008

On June 13, 2008, I was in Aix en Provence, France, officiating at the wedding of Meredith Scott and David Pfeffer, when we got word that Tim Russert had died.

Tim was the highly respected host of NBC's *Meet the Press*. The Russerts had been vacationing in Italy. Tim had left his wife, Maureen, and son, Luke, a couple of days early to get back home for his Sunday show. He had a cardiac arrest while at the office.

Even though I had planned a two-week stay in Europe following the wedding, the only thing I could think was that I had to get back to Washington. As any clergyperson will tell you, when any parishioners or friends die, your best-laid plans take a backseat. The bride's mother, Jeannie Rutherfoord, whose sons were all my students, arranged for me to fly home immediately with the bride's father, Jim Scott, on his private plane.

Luke, too, was one of my students. Tim and Maureen were "on-duty parents" devoted to their son and the school. Tim was particularly popular with the boys at St. Albans, rarely missing any of Luke's football games and frequently giving them a "shout out" on his show.

The Russerts were Roman Catholic. There is a wonderful story told about Tim, who when he discovered he was going to be a father, promised God he would attend Mass every Sunday if the baby had a safe delivery. Tim stayed true to his promise.

I knew the St. Albans community would somehow also want to pay respect to Tim. Because of the worldwide reaction to his death, in consultation with Maureen and Luke, it was decided we would have the visitation the day before the funeral at the school. Tim's body would "lie in state" in the refectory. Our public spaces at the school would be large enough to handle the thousands of people who would come to pay their respects, including President George W. Bush and First Lady Laura Bush. The lines of mourners included fans from around the United States, old friends from Buffalo, and the nation's most prominent journalists and politicians. It stretched the entire day around the Cathedral Close out to Wisconsin Avenue and down Massachusetts Avenue.

Perhaps the most moving thing of all was the devotion of Luke's friends to Tim. They devised a way to have an "honor guard" at the head and foot of his coffin, taking turns standing at attention throughout the length of the visitation, which was carried live on CNN.

To me, this was the St. Albans family at its most loving and best. Regardless of celebrity or diversity, as any of our families and alumni will tell you, the St. Albans School community reacts the same way. We celebrate together. We grieve together. We worship together. Over the years, and after all we've been through, it is who we have become.

The Goldfinch

The Little Sanctuary at St. Albans School was built during the tenure of Bishop Henry Yates Satterlee, the first Episcopal Bishop of Washington, so there might be a place to worship on Mount St. Alban while the cathedral was being constructed. The Jerusalem Altar, Canterbury Pulpit, and Bishop's Chair were all installed there until it was time for them to be moved into the cathedral. In 1909 it became a chapel for the students at St. Albans. It is an oddly shaped building, as it has had to be expanded over the years to make room for a growing student body.

Its treasures include an iron pulpit fashioned from a piece of the battleship *Maine* and an ebony likeness of Jesus sent by a tribe in Africa when the boys raised money for the purchase of a motorcycle for their missionary priest. Many windows, some of which depict the trial of Saint Alban, were designed by the renowned stained glass artisan Rowan LeCompte and his wife, Irene. Interestingly, those windows include orcs, the malevolent characters from J. R. R. Tolkien's *The Hobbit* and *Lord of the Rings*, which were introduced into the school curriculum by the late school chaplain, the Reverend Craig Eder. One of those windows is dedicated to the martyrdoms of Saint Alban and President John F. Kennedy, whose nephew Edward attended St. Albans.

If you look closely, the Little Sanctuary also has a goldfinch.

At the end of the school year, the students in the Lower School regularly gather to watch a slide show of their year in pictures. A few years ago, only days before the slide show was to occur, the students had suffered the loss of one of their own, a C-Former who along with his parents and housekeeper had been the victims of a violent crime.

As the students gathered in the Little Sanctuary, a goldfinch flew in the door with them and landed on a beam above their heads. It remained there the entire length of the slide show, and as the boys left, it flew out with them.

Later, the Lower School chaplain was recounting the story to a school parent who was a close friend of the boy's family and who, along with them, attended the Greek Orthodox Church. She explained that in their religious tradition, Mary, the mother of Jesus, is often depicted holding a goldfinch, which represents the passion of Christ.

A tiny carved goldfinch now sits on a beam in the Little Sanctuary directly above the boys' heads.

Cornerstone Garden

For many years I had hoped we would build a columbarium or memorial garden at St. Albans for the interment of people's ashes. So when Carol and Leonard Steuart made a gift to the school for such "holy ground," I was thrilled.

Designed by St. Albans alumni Richard Williams, it is a beautiful terraced garden with bluestone walls that lies between the Little Sanctuary and the Lane Johnson Building. While it was being constructed, the cornerstone of the school was uncovered behind an enormous bank of forsythia, which flourished after the former chaplain, Craig Eder, planted a tiny plant outside the window of his office in the 1970s. On the cornerstone are written the words from Psalm 21:4:

> He asked life of thee;
> thou gavest it to him,
> length of days for ever and ever.

After its completion, it was dedicated as the Cornerstone Garden in a beautiful service. Immediately after the dedication, I was walking through the garden with Carol and Leonard when a soccer ball came flying from out of the lower school playground across Pilgrim Road (known as the prison yard because of the high cyclone fence) and landed smack in the middle of the plantings Carol had painstakingly instructed the gardeners to plant. Carol feigned horror and Leonard fell out laughing. It is also a place for frequent games of hide-and-seek.

The names of alumni, faculty, and staff now adorn its walls, many of my friends, students, and colleagues among them. Now sadly they include Leonard's who, never losing his sense of humor, called me weekly after the dedication to see "how sign-ups were going." The garden is somewhat narrow, as it is between buildings. I know Leonard would love to know that one day two boys in the C Form (4th grade) asked, "Mr. Billow, are they going to bury people standing up?"

A SELECTION OF HOMILIES
Ben Hutto
St. John's Episcopal Church, Washington, DC
During Christmas of 2014, I got a call from Ben Hutto while on vacation. The news wasn't good. Ben was the Director of Performing Arts at

the Cathedral Schools and a dear colleague and friend of mine. He had been diagnosed with gallbladder cancer. It is known as an "orphan cancer" because it is so rare and very little is known about it. What is known is that once you realize you have it, very little can be done about it.

Not enough can be said about Ben and his influence on the musical lives of thousands of people. Below is the eulogy I preached at his funeral:

In a poem by Joyce Sutphen titled "The One True Choir," the author speaks of a director that brings out the beauty of the blended voices of a choir.

For many of us that will be a lasting memory of Ben Hutto, for those of us who sang for him and those of us who from behind watched his animated figure directing four or four hundred voices together in harmony.

He had more energy than anyone I ever knew . . . and more patience. All due respect to the clergy present . . . God love him . . . he had to sit through the same sermons not once, but twice, sometimes three times on any given Sunday morning.

You may be surprised to learn his intended career was journalism, but as fate would have it he chose to forego his scholarship at a prestigious graduate school and return to Charleston to teach English at Porter-Gaud. In true English teacher fashion, a couple of weeks ago when Luis Leon suggested a Gospel reading for this service, Ben said, "No, because it ends in a preposition." It was at Porter-Gaud that music took hold, and lucky for us, the rest is history.

Ben left Charleston—but Charleston never left Ben. Nobody had more fun or could tell a funnier story about the eccentricities of Charlestonians.

Rumor has it he was a liberal . . . and a Democrat.

If you knew Ben you know he was passionate about civil rights. While growing up he had a white neighbor who was a racist. Ben and a friend called all the black funeral homes in Charleston, gave them the address of the man (who was very much alive), and asked them to pick up his body. By the time the last hearse arrived, all the neighbors who had gathered on their porches to see what was going on heard the man yell (expletive deleted), "I'm not dead!" Mission accomplished. I only wish Ben were here to embellish the story.

Ironically, stories Ben loved came from a book entitled Being Dead Is No Excuse: The Official Southern Ladies Guide to Hosting the Perfect Funeral. *There is actually, along with what and what not to serve at receptions, a chapter on hymns to avoid at all costs.*

Funny, but the truth is Ben was not a musical snob, as evidenced by the diversity of his taste. Luis and I have concurred he was the perfect *church organist because his first priority was the pastoral care of all of you, with requests ranging from the Redskins' fight song to "Somewhere Over the Rainbow."*

And just imagine what a day in his life was like between St. John's, the Cathedral Schools, the Royal School of Church Music, weddings, funerals, from Bach to Rogers and Hammerstein to Thomas Tallis and back again.

What a gifted and wonderful man, introducing music to literally thousands of children, many of whom have chosen it as a career. And with regard to performance, imagine—unlike an actor or performer or a preacher—Ben spent his life with his back *to his audience.*

And true to his nature the performance was never about him—it was always about bringing forth the beauty in each member of the choir or orchestra. And if that isn't living [in] the footsteps of Jesus, I don't know what is! Since Jesus's singular goal is to bring forth the true voice and beauty in each of us.

Ben's view of his ministry is best expressed in his own words found in a letter he wrote to his congregation at Christ Episcopal Church in Charlotte:

"Music is, I believe, one of the Church's great missionary opportunities. In its transmission, it has meaning for the faithful, for the faithless, and for those who have lost their faith. It is a mission whose spirit can be expressed in the home by the family singing Christmas Carols, or in the most magnificent ecclesiastical structure, by a highly trained choir. It knows no social, intellectual, or sectarian barriers. It expresses our loftiest ideals, our deepest emotions. It is one of the gifts

of God which reminds us that we are above the other creatures of God but lower than the angels."

So gentleman! Tuck in your shirts and straighten your ties! Ladies and gentlemen, heads up*! Smile! Sing out! Sopranos, alto, tenors, and basses! Find your true voice! Sing out for justice and joy and ham biscuits! Sing out for Ben!*

For in Ben's eyes and in the eyes of God . . . We are "The One True Choir."

Amen.

Laura Houghteling
Washington National Cathedral

Last week John Mastny, a recent graduate of St. Albans, was murdered, the victim of a street robbery in Berkeley, California. In his apartment he had a photograph album of a Russian exchange trip he took as a freshman at St. Albans. In it was a group shot and ironically there was John with his arm around Laura, a graduate of National Cathedral School, also a murder victim here in Bethesda some months ago. As was Laura's, John's service will also be in the cathedral tomorrow.

The community of the Cathedral Schools are reeling, as they feel robbed of two of our most brilliant and promising graduates, and we extend our sympathies to both the Mastny and Houghteling families.

I taught both Laura and John. Among my most treasured possessions are what the young people call their "Philo papers"—philosophies of life in which the kids are required to articulate their beliefs and substantiate why they believe as they do. Susanna Mulroney will read you an excerpt from Laura's paper.

Science teachers tell us that we live our lives in a dynamic, not static world. The children remind me of that every day. They are always growing and changing. Through the course of "Philo" I could see the evolution of Laura's thought. That was six years ago. I can only imagine where her studies at Harvard took her.

In this universe there are forces which are beyond our control. Evil forces which manifest themselves in, of all things, people. People of the Christian faith attribute evil to a being they name Satan. Laura, in her Philo project, told what it was she would use to confront evil. It was Love. The greatest force among the powers and principalities Saint Paul described in his letter to the Corinthians. It was love that Christ used in confronting those who would take his life.

Let love be Laura's legacy.

Into God's kingdom of light and love we commit Laura, messenger of love on this All Saints' Day.

John Mastny
Washington National Cathedral

"I need, more than my children need me, a way of seeing in the dark. I cannot call it ordained of God. I cannot get that far."

That is one of the concluding lines of Dr. Dysart in Peter Shaffer's play, Equus. *John Mastny spoke those lines himself in a brilliant re-creation of the role right here on the stage of Trapier Theater some months ago.*

I cannot call John's murder "ordained of God."

Those of us here who are teachers recognize when the spark ignites and our children burn with the desire to learn. Quoting another line from that play, John "knew a passion more fierce than I have ever known," and it manifested itself here at St. Albans in drama, poetry, and dance.

John's light burned with such intensity, many of us remember specific moments . . . such as his performance in Equus. *Frankie Tacker remembers him most vividly as Mercutio in* Romeo and Juliet. *He was extraordinarily enthusiastic about so many things. And his passion led him into what T. S. Eliot would call "the labyrinthian ways of his own mind."*

Consider his passion for Carmina Burana, *which proved to be prophetic. John sought reason for existence and he found his response to "empty fate" in dance, which he celebrated with his beloved girlfriend, Libby. Much of John's philosophic thought is found in a paper he wrote for my class in which he included his poem "The Dervish Song, 1888," a tribute to Nijinsky. Here is a quote from the conclusion of the poem, also prophetic:*

> *The body remained*
> *Turned to dust*
>
> *The body dies but the soul lives*
>
> *He is dancing, dancing over corpses*
> *Past the parched battlefield*
> *Turning, turning, dancing on,*
> *Whirling, whirling through space,*
> *Leaping across the face of God*
> *Absorbed, freed in his eternal dance.*

Thanks be to God for the life of John now freed in his eternal dance.

Amen

The Day John Selinger Walked on Water
A Homily for John Selinger, Friend and Business Manager of STA

As you might imagine, John gave Ann many instructions throughout their life together, some of which she followed. Most recently, he told her that under no circumstances was she to put in his obituary that he died "after a long illness."

It is much better said that John Selinger died after having a fabulous life.

And John would love it that this comment has inspired a homily! And a short one!

But think for a moment, how much of the Gospels involve the circumstances surrounding Jesus's death?! Most of it. Theologians agree that most of Jesus's life is totally unknown to us, and what a shame that is. It is true that people—even the apostles—didn't understand just who he was until the resurrection. Then, they had to reconstruct his life.

Much in the same way, we will be doing in the reception following this service, and the years to come: Reconstructing John's life!

He'd really love it that I'm comparing him to Jesus.

But celebrate his life—the stories are endless. One of my favorites is at an engagement reception. John, with an entire plate of food in one hand and a drink in the other, stepped onto what John described as a beautiful blue dance floor (which actually happened to be the cover of a swimming pool) and walked the entire length of the pool as the cover sank, and didn't spill a drop. He stepped out of the pool and took a bow as tables around the pool applauded—elegance, class, sophistication. Guy Steuart told me it was the night John Selinger walked on water. So the comparisons with Jesus are endless!

So, Amy and Johnny, have no fear! The Gospels your children will hear will get better with time! There are eyewitness accounts of parables, aphorisms, miracles, and unconditional love.

Always remember the word gospel *means good news and the good news is that we had John Selinger in our lives.*

John Selinger—who died after having a fabulous life.

Amen.

Upon the Death of Ryan White

Yesterday was Palm Sunday. It is marked by Jesus's triumphant entry into Jerusalem with people waving palm branches. It seems they were thinking, "Hooray! He's here! The Messiah! He'll get rid of the Romans and restore Israel."

But to the more cautious observer, looming in the back of one or two of the apostles' minds might have been his warning that the messiah "would suffer and die and on the third day rise."

The people of Jerusalem had to face it. Jesus wasn't going to be some great military leader. The Zealots' disappointment in him probably had something to do with why the people voted to release Barabbas.

What would Jesus accomplish by peaceful means? Barabbas will take up arms, will defeat the Romans.

So I dare say the Israelites got what they wanted, the Romans didn't. Barabbas had murdered a Roman soldier.

Jesus, in his infinite wisdom, knew what he had to go through in order to convince people he was who he said he was.

Now why he didn't save himself from torture and death only he knows, but here's a question: If he didn't die, would we really know how much God loves us?

God could be some great puppeteer, pulling all the strings from up above. Instead he cut all the strings, jumped down from the rafters, and got right on the stage with us. He knows what we're going through and told us he would be with us even though life is really tough at times. And he knows because it got really tough for him.

His friends betrayed him; he got beaten and crucified.

Three days later a reported resurrection.

His response? No matter what happens to you in your life, I love you. I will be with you. Nothing can separate you from my love—not even death.

This week I wish he would have saved Ryan White, the boy from Indiana who had AIDS. But he didn't. At least not in the way I might have imagined.

Sometimes God doesn't do what we want God to do, or be whom we want God to be.

Sometimes God turns out to do and be something better.

A Tribute to STA Mother and Grandmother Bette Catoe Strudwick, MD

We have just heard the reading of Jesus before Pilate.

You know, I've always wondered why Pontius Pilate has been so vilified over the centuries. After all, he "washed his hands" of Jesus's death, didn't surrender to the will of the people.

Here we have Jesus—who just yesterday (Palm Sunday) was the darling of the people—very popular.

"Hosanna! Hosanna!" Folks are waving palm branches.

Then in the twinkling of an eye, they turned on him yelling, "Crucify him! Crucify him!"

What happened? He disappointed them for some reason? He didn't turn out as they expected?

This scene shows the problem with mob mentality—can you relate?

Like maybe when somebody becomes irrational at a ballgame and stats yelling "Throw the bum out!" Or even in victory, when folks smash cars, and torch them. What's that about?!

Several years ago, a friend was coaching a T-ball game at Turtle Park. There was a call some of the moms did, and didn't, agree with. They started hitting one another with umbrellas!

Another example . . .

There is a great scene in Monty Python's The Life of Brian, *where they're listening to Jesus give the Sermon on the Mount and they're so far away they're having trouble hearing him correctly. Jesus is saying, "Blessed are the peacemakers."*

Someone says, "What's he saying?"

Someone answers, "Blessed are the cheese makers."

Another says, "Well, not just the cheese makers, but manufacturers of any dairy products."

Well, frustration grows. Someone yells, "Shut up, Big Nose!" And a fistfight ensues . . .

Ridiculous, right?

It's comical really, unless it turns bad like in real life—like in Jesus's case.

Ever been in a mob?

Would you step up?

A great friend of mine, and an STA mother and grandmother, Dr. Bette Catoe Strudwick, is a renowned African-American pediatrician here in DC. Her mother was a White House pastry chef. Her father owned and operated a taxicab. She graduated from Howard University Medical School in 1951. She began her practice operating out of her basement in DC.

Last year, during our Epiphany series at St. Albans, she told a story about finding herself in the middle of the riots in DC after the assassination of Dr. Martin Luther King in 1968. She had gone to pick up her mother and was driving home when she found herself in the middle of a mob burning and turning over cars. Suddenly they surrounded her car. Bette, a slight woman with nerves of steel, at great personal risk, got out of her car, put her hands on her hips, stared those boys down, ordered them off her car, and told them to "go home!"

They listened.

My advice to you—if you find yourself in a mob:

Be brave.

Be Dr. Bette Catoe Strudwick.

And you just might be able to prevent . . . a crucifixion.

Now go in peace to love and serve the Lord.

Who's the Crazy One?

How do we know what to believe?

I have:

- *a friend who claims he can fly (without benefit of plane)*
- *a friend who claims crystals heal*
- *a friend who claims to have seen a spaceship*
- *a friend who claims an out-of-body experience*
- *a friend who claims to have seen ghosts*

You might wonder about my associations! Yet, who am I to talk?

I believe a God—one that in human form walked the earth—performed miracles, was crucified, died, and rose from the dead?!

Who's the crazy one?

How do we decide what's legit and what isn't? You tell me.

Some of you guys say to me, "You should be able to believe whatever you want to, as long as nobody gets hurt."

Well, I'm not willing to go quite that far, and cults do scare me, particularly in the way people are manipulated. Interestingly enough, the earliest Christians were viewed as a cult, by those who were not Christian.

And let's be realistic—if your friend came home and said something about eating body and blood, you'd say, "What?"

So what do we do?

Well, before you say this crazy stuff isn't an issue for me, it just may be.

Four out of the five people I described in the beginning were Episcopalians; the fifth was Presbyterian. The person who believes in the power of crystals, or the spaceship, may be sitting next to you in the pew. Actually, that's what I like about being an Episcopalian. It's also the reason we're criticized, for being too liberal—too permissive—we're some kind of collection trying to figure out what we're to make of all this stuff, including the "woo-woo."

We use in analysis what are called the three pillars: scripture, tradition (people have wrestled with this stuff before us), and reason. And we pray to Jesus (the one thing we all agree on) and ask him to reveal what is legit and what isn't. And we trust his will be done.

The one thing we don't want to do is close our minds so that we aren't open to things of the spirit—as happened to the people in Jesus's hometown. Just because something is unsettling is not a good enough reason to dismiss it. Use the three pillars. Pray about it.

Healing power in crystals, out-of-body experience—what's the big deal about that? Imagine if the neighbor kid, the carpenter's son, claimed to be God.

And he was.

Mebane, North Carolina
An STA Chapel Talk on Religious Diversity

Many of you know, I have a dog.

His name is Mebane; that's spelled M-E-B-A-N-E. He's named for the town where he was found—Mebane, North Carolina. A buddy of mine has a furniture company there and he was building a new plant. One of the bulldozers moved a pile of wood and three puppies jumped out. Craig took one and named him Mebane.

He's a beautiful dog, and people are always asking me what kind he is. The vet told me he's an All-American—I think that means he's a mutt.

A couple of weeks ago, the Westminster Kennel Club dog show was on TV. Some of you might have seen it—hundreds of dogs from all over the country in a purebred competition. It's a riot to watch. Unfortunately, Mebane wouldn't qualify. "Best of Mutt" isn't a category, but I love him anyway.

It's interesting to me how purebred stuff going on at the Westminster Kennel Club transcends other aspects of our lives; i.e., socially it's better to be a snooty "Longbottom" from Boston than it is a hayseed "Haybacket" from Culpeper (those are made-up names). But the truth is, some of the Boston Longbottoms would just as soon trade places with the Haybackets and spend their summer evenings fishing on the Rapidan rather than be at a white-tie ball at the Isabella Stewart Gardner Museum. Ironically, some Haybackets dream of escaping the confines of their small Virginia town—where karaoke night at Bull Durham's is the place to be.

The same thing goes on religiously. Historically, the hierarchy of some churches have taught religious purity is the only acceptable way. For some, it's better to be a purebred Christian, Jew, or Muslim, or even more astounding, even within the same faith, there are those who claim their denomination is the only way. What's that about?

One of the most misinterpreted passages in scripture is in our own Gospel of John when Jesus says, "I am the Way, the Truth, and the Life; no one comes to the Father but by Me." First of all, if you do your homework, there are some serious questions about whether or not Jesus really said it; secondly, if he did, he didn't say if you're Jewish, Hindu, or Muslim, you're toast.

He's saying at some point in your religious journey, you will encounter him. In another passage he says, "I have other sheep who are not of this fold"—just what did he mean by that?

So I guess what I'm saying is many of us are what Mitch Albom calls "religious mutts." Trying to find truth in all religions, I've told you before, Jesus's teachings work for me, but never once is he quoted as saying you cannot find great insights from other religions.

Don't fall into the trap that some cultural, religious, ethnic, animal breeders would have you believe—that Fifi is better than Mebane, 'cause I know in my heart it just isn't true.

Football Camp Homily
Camp Paddy Run

I've been reading a book this summer for the new Philo course called Pilgrim Souls. *It's a collection of spiritual autobiographies—Moses, Socrates, Eldridge Cleaver, a real assortment. I've been struck by a couple of things: that they're totally overwhelmed by something far greater than themselves, and their desire to let go of themselves and be lost in God.*

Reminding me of Jesus's saying, "Whoever would lose himself for my sake will find himself."

This is an important analogy for all of you—far greater than any one of you is this team.

No one of you is more important than any other. Like the lesson said, we are all members of one body, and if you don't believe it, try going without water.

When I was your age, I spent a lot of time on the bench, but time and again the guys on the first string said they were inspired by my support, and my effort, and my commitment. They made amazing plays because they knew somebody cared.

So, lose yourself—in this team—see where it takes you.

I predict few things in your life will have as strong an impact as being on a team.

And you'll begin to understand how in losing yourself, you find yourself.

Consider the Lilies
A Thank-You to St. Albans School Altar Guild

Consider the lilies of the field; they neither toil nor spin yet I tell you even Solomon in all his glory was not arrayed as one of these.

*—*LUKE 12:27

We're grateful to all of you who work with the lilies and maybe you, more than anyone else, remain aware of God's handiwork.

I think we go blithely along here taking flowers for granted, but let them not be there one day and everyone notices.

Sort of like being a mom—especially at dinnertime.

When I was in seminary, there was a lady there named Annilee T. Brown—hostess—who made a life of caring for her boys. There were women there, but she didn't like them much.

Her door was always open to us and to everyone who came to the seminary. Much of Annilee we took for granted, as you might a mom, but the things that she did with flowers and meals told of one who lived in expectation of the boys she loved.

This is the way a Christian is to live in expectation of Christ.

When I was in England a few years back, I was out in the countryside and came upon this little church that looked as though it had long since been abandoned. The roof was falling in, but the hinges on the door worked and the flowers were beautifully arranged.

And that's all I needed.

So, thank you for this that you do and for what it means for helping to keep expectation alive in me and in the boys you love.

Following September 11, 2001

In all my years on this earth, I've never fully resigned myself to the deaths of those I have loved.

As a priest I've been at the bedside of many who have died and I have marveled at people's bravery as they have faced the inevitable, but still I have never quite resigned myself to the fact that they are really gone . . . if they really are.

Sure, physically they are gone. But the people I have loved live on, in my heart and mind.

And maybe, just maybe, that is what Easter is all about—and what resurrection is all about.

I've never seen anyone literally raised from the dead, but maybe what I'm experiencing is what the apostles experienced when the Gospel states "their eyes were opened" and they "saw Jesus in the breaking of the bread." The ritual brought him back to them and he lived on in their hearts.

As he does for so many to this day . . .

When I am doing something that we did together, many of the people I have loved live on in my heart and mind.

Maybe that is why I am not resigned.

The Gospel of Alex
Homily upon the Death of Alexander Nimr Maasry, STA '99, Washington National Cathedral

For Alex:

The word gospel *means "good news." If we were to write the Gospel of Alex, we would begin as did the writers of the Gospels of Jesus, reconstructing a life to find the enormous meaning in it.*

That is in fact what we are beginning to do today, hearing the stories of Lenny, Rob, and George. Hearing from them what it was about Alex that transformed their lives.

If I were to write my version of the Gospel of Alex, Chapter 1, Verse 1 would begin right here on the Cathedral Close. It seemed to me almost as long as I was at St. Albans we had a Maasry there. Every couple of years a new one would appear. Even without an introduction you would know who they were because they looked just alike.

The Reverend Claudia Gould reminded me Paul Herman, the head of the Lower School, greeted each child by name at the beginning of every year and if he couldn't remember their names they would get a dollar. The Maasrys cleaned up! George, nope, Alex, nope, Caesar!

My office was in the corner of what was then the "new wing" with a big window to the right of my desk that looked out on the Senior Circle. The Maasry boys would often drop in. George just to visit, Caesar generally had a purpose of some sort. And then there was Alex. Have you ever had the feeling someone was staring at you . . . and they are? That would be Alex, every day staring in at the window, catching me unaware, making a stern headmaster-like face.

You boys will remember what was known as Mr. Heischman's "look."
Then around the corner Alex would come laughing.

What I wouldn't do to have that face appear one more time.

The Gospels in the Bible record that after his death Jesus appeared
to the apostles in the "breaking of the bread." To this day that is a
ritual we continue to remind us to carry out Jesus's work in the world.

So too we have the chance to have Alex's spirit live on with the
work of the Alex Maasry Foundation. Just as the scripture says the
apostles' "eyes were opened," the foundation will "open eyes" to the
need for civic engagement in effecting social change. It will keep alive
the spirit of a young man who truly believed he was his "brother's
keeper."

Many of us here were his teachers. As a teacher you try to gage
how class is going by the looks on your students' faces. There's the bored
look, the bewildered look, the asleep look, and the "get me out of here"
look. But you hope every once in a while the lightbulb will go on and
something they read will lead them to discover their "calling." Fred-
erick Buechner speaks to this in his definition of vocation in his book
Wishful Thinking: A Theological ABC, *a book Alex was* supposed
to have read in my class. He says if you follow your heart, you will
make a difference in this world. Alex did.

So now let's begin Chapter 2 of the Gospel of Alex.
Amen.

There are so many things we would like to save our children from, but
we can't. One of the great honors of my job is being present for the life
passages of the young men and women entrusted to my care. It might be
assumed my pastoral responsibilities would end with their high school
graduations, but that has not been the case. And it has been my greatest
privilege to have known the students, parents, faculty, staff, and the gen-
erations of their families and to have been present through the profound
moments of their lives. Over the years, the following Bernadine Healy
quote has meant a great deal to me:

As a physician who has been deeply privileged to share the most profound moments of people's lives, including their final moments, let me tell you a secret. People facing death don't think about what degrees they have earned, what positions they have held, or how much wealth they have accumulated.

At the end, what really matters is who you loved and who loved you. The circle of love is everything and is a good measure of a past life. It is the gift of greatest worth.

Washington National Cathedral

THE NATIONAL CATHEDRAL SITS HIGH ATOP MOUNT ST. ALBAN IN THE city of Washington, DC. The land was a gift of the Glover family, and in 1893 the cathedral was chartered by Congress to be a "House of Prayer for All People." It is surrounded by the three Cathedral Schools—the National Cathedral School for Girls; St. Albans, the National Cathedral School for Boys; and Beauvoir, the National Cathedral Elementary School—as well as the College of Preachers.

All of the cathedral institutions fall under the governance structure of the Protestant Episcopal Cathedral Foundation (PECF), and each has its own Board of Governors and development offices.

As chaplain of St. Albans, I for many years served as a volunteer at the cathedral, serving on the regular Sunday and weekday rotation of services as well as officiating at major school events, weddings, baptisms, and funerals for students and their families.

I also taught an A Form (6th grade) course called Cathedral Faith, which offered me the challenge of shepherding forty-five little boys through the cathedral twice a week. As a result, I made very dear friends on the cathedral staff to whom I am devoted.

AN APPOINTMENT WITH THE VERGER

John Kraus was a close friend and, for many years, the verger of the cathedral. For those who might not know, the verger is the master of ceremonies. For his part, John carried a magnificent silver and ebony verge. To be the verger is an enormous job with great responsibility and it is done with great reverence and formality—greeting presidents, heads of state, kings, queens, dignitaries, and the like.

If you ever saw John presiding in person or on TV, he never cracked a smile, but behind the scenes he had a hilarious sense of humor. He needed it, having to deal with the self-important nature of some church leaders and folks in Washington. I think he would have loved the fact that children would often mistakenly refer to him as the cathedral "virgin."

The story I want to tell, however, is not about mishaps during a service (of which there were many— like the time the boys knocked over the baptismal font while racing out at graduation) but a story John told me that has to do with the verger as keeper of the cathedral records.

One day years ago, John received a call from an elderly woman who by name he recognized as one of the most prominent figures in Washington society. She asked if she could make an appointment to come see him, and he of course obliged. They were to meet in the cathedral slype. When she and her assistant arrived, she asked her assistant to be excused. When John shut the door, the woman said, "Mr. Kraus, it is time to change the name of my son's father in the baptismal registry."

Another great story John told me involved two bishops of the church attending the funeral of a fellow bishop in the nave of the cathedral. As they listened to the eulogy, one quipped to the other, "One person lying in the nave is sufficient."

I was enormously honored that John left written instructions that I be the officiant at his funeral. He also asked specifically that there be no eulogy. When John died the "powers that be" determined that the bishop would be the officiant and instructed me to give the eulogy. Under the circumstances, I did the best I could. It was titled "A Eulogy That Isn't a Eulogy: A Thanksgiving for the Life of John Kraus."

THE A FORM CLASS

We used the cathedral as our textbook. We learned about American history, world history, and church history as depicted in all of its artistry— the stonework, needlework, woodwork, and stained glass.

Favorites of the boys were the wood sculptures of the apostles at the high altar, each holding the instrument of their *death*; the stained

I told the boys if they didn't behave, I'd take their picture as evidence.

glass in the war memorial chapel, which depicted paratroopers, the landings at Normandy, and the Battle of Midway; the pennies in the floor in the Lincoln Bay, with one penny face-down representing South Carolina, the first state to secede from the Union; and their number one favorite, the memorial a cathedral woodcarver left to his son who was killed in the Second World War. It is of a lion with a snake in its mouth. The lion represents the Allied forces, and the snake has the face of Adolf Hitler.

Their final exam was to take their parents on a guided tour, with the parents filling in the blanks on a sheet of paper as the boys explained what they were seeing.

One year I heard a dad say, "Really?! George Washington is buried here??"

After hearing that, I can only imagine what some of the parents thought of me as a teacher.

It was always a challenge leading classes of forty-five little boys around such an enormous space with all of its nooks, crannies, stairwells, buttresses, and balconies. There are a million places to hide, and they did—and they could run a lot faster. Once in a while in their excitement, they'd get ahead of me, particularly in the stairwells to the towers. We weren't particularly popular with a couple of the cathedral docents, who were known as "the purple ladies."

One year when we were going up the north tower stairway, one of the boys shot ahead of me. As I rounded the corner, I looked up and saw a purple lady had the boy by the arm. She said in a very firm voice, "Stop running—this is not your home!" Then I heard his little voice say, "Yes it is. Bishop Walker told us so."

Effi Barry Funeral

Pat Elwood, a friend and a St. Albans mother, was for a time chief of protocol for the Washington, DC, mayor's office. She called and explained that Effi Barry, the former wife of former DC mayor Marion Barry, had died. Effi had been a St. Albans mom while her son, Christopher, had attended the Lower School. Pat had contacted the cathedral arrangements office several times, and they had not returned her calls. She wondered if I could help.

When I called over there, I got a very nice young woman on the phone who had never heard of Mrs. Barry and wasn't sure if she qualified to have her service there. I then called Steve Huber, the vicar of the cathedral, also a friend, who immediately said "of course."

Steve and I co-officiated at the funeral. It was a beautiful service, and the Washington establishment turned out for a lovely and gracious woman who had endured very public scandals involving her husband. After her divorce from the mayor, Effie taught at Hampton University in Virginia until her death at sixty-three from leukemia.

The former mayor gave a moving tribute for his former wife, as did Christopher.

The cathedral is a very interesting space in which to worship. Experience dictates what works and does not work, particularly with regard to music and sound. And all events are carefully choreographed by the vergers, who are very stern about what is and is not allowed.

No one was expecting what Mary Wilson of the Supremes did when she sang her tribute "for Effi." She removed the microphone from its stand and walked down the steps and around the coffin while singing "Lush Life."

As you might imagine, Steve and I would not make eye contact with the vergers. They were not amused. I have to confess, for Steve and me it "made" the funeral. After all, it was Mary Wilson of the Supremes.

THE LITURGICAL POLICE

This seems as good a time as any to talk about those in the church that fancy themselves "liturgical police." Sometimes they are on the staff, but more often than not are volunteers. They are self-appointed liturgists and make up their own rules, sniffing their noses at changes often made in the liturgy or dress for practical or pastoral reasons. The cathedral over the years has had no shortage of them. Often the bishop or dean must intervene.

I remember one year I requested a processional cross for "beating the bounds" of the Cathedral Close on Rogation Sunday. I was informed by a verger at the time that "the processional cross was to never leave the building." That was, until the bishop requested it.

One year a widow asked if the white vestments at her husband's funeral could have a floral pattern. Request denied.

The worst was when a C-Former at St. Albans was killed in a car accident and his classmates requested we sing his favorite song, Three Dog Night's "Joy to the World." Again denied, until the bishop got wind of it.

I remember the Reverend Dr. Charles "Charlie" Price, my theology professor, quoting Martin Luther: "If you're going to sin, sin boldly!" You've got to be doing it for the right reasons. Although there are purists among us, clergy are always bending liturgical rules, particularly for pastoral reasons. I confess to being one of them, allowing a favorite song in a time of grief, a favorite reading in a time of joy. Charlie, who incidentally contributed much of the 1979 Book of Common Prayer, allowed that, as there are 522 occurrences of the word *may* in the prayer book, it gives you some leeway, thank God.

The most volatile encounter with the "liturgical police" involved a St. Albans graduation, as recounted below.

THE BAPTISMAL FONT

In his address to graduating seniors, the headmaster of St. Albans reminds the young men they will perhaps never be a part of a service as grand as their graduation ceremony in the nave of the Washington National Cathedral, and certain behavior is expected of them.

This service has all the pomp of a coronation, with trumpeters and choirs. The faculty process in their academic gowns along with members of the fiftieth reunion class. The graduates follow in matching khakis and blue blazers. After prayers and the requisite commencement address, they receive their diplomas from the Bishop of Washington with a thousand of their friends and family watching.

The one tradition that occurs under the disapproving eyes of *some* members of the cathedral staff is the graduates are allowed to cheer and race out of the cathedral during the retiring recessional.

Several years ago, the cathedral placed an enormous stone baptismal font in the center of the aisle. This created a bit of an obstacle for the seventy boys, who carefully rehearsed their exit so as not to run into the font. The cathedral staff said the large font would be moved to the side before commencement.

As the recessional began, the boys picked up their pace, breaking into a run a third of the way down the aisle. As they approached the crossing and saw the baptismal font still there, they made their way around it on either side. But, as fate would have it, one graduate, a 250-pound tackle on the football team, hit it full force, knocking it off its pedestal, and sent it smashing to the marble floor.

After the service, headmaster Vance Wilson and I received a tongue lashing from a cathedral staff member furious that a priceless artifact had been destroyed by this ridiculous tradition. Vance and I walked over to the place where it fell to inspect the damage, expecting the worst. In the middle of the aisle lay the font, upside down. There was a sticker on the bottom. It read "Pier 1."

The tradition continues.

SERVING ON THE PECF

I was in my first year of retirement and had just arrived in Los Angeles for a vacation when the Right Reverend John Chane, the Episcopal Bishop of Washington, called and said, "Will, I want you to serve on the Foundation Board."

Me: "Oh no, Bishop, I . . ."

The bishop: "Oh, yes you will!"

Enough said. I was canonically resident in the diocese and bound to be "obedient," as I had pledged in my ordination vows.

I was aware several of my close friends were serving on the board: Vance Wilson (my former boss), Richard Schoenfeld, Steve McGregor, Geoffrey Baker, and Julie Miller, all of whom had been board chairs at St. Albans, and Llewellyn Bensfield, whose children I had baptized while at St. Columba's many years earlier.

The Protestant Episcopal Cathedral Foundation (PECF) board oversees all of the institutions on the Cathedral Close. The Bishop said I would be there to represent the interest of the schools, not to contribute my expert financial advice, which was a relief because such advice from me is nonexistent.

During my tenure, for me the most important thing to remember was something I taught my A Form classes. The children learned that the tomb of the Right Reverend Henry Yates Satterlee, the first Bishop of Washington, rests on the foundation stone. That stone reads "And the Word was made flesh and dwelt among us."

The Word made flesh is Jesus. His life and teachings need to remain central to the mission of the cathedral.

THE BOOK OF BILL

From 1992 to 2008 Bill Petersen was a cathedral verger who then became head of the cathedral arrangements office. He was beloved by the people with whom he worked and was well known for his sense of humor and his hilarious insights. He loved to poke fun at the cathedral clergy, staff, and volunteers, some of whom can be a bit officious.

For years Stephen Pearcy, a fellow staff member, kept a log of Bill's quips and comments. Upon his death, Stephen read them to fellow staff members, resulting in gales of laughter. He gave out copies. It is known by those of us who loved him as "The Book of Bill." Here are just a few examples.

Recalling questions from callers: "When does the eleven o'clock service begin?" "Is the four o'clock service still at four o'clock this week?" And the astounding "Is Christmas on the twenty-fifth of December again?"

Discussing priests recalcitrant about being at worship services, particularly at the cathedral: "In seminary, they need to have a class where they say, 'Sundays—those are the days we work.'"

When told that a cathedral canon would not be present on Christmas Eve: "You would think a priest would realize he has to work on Christmas."

On finding priests for Easter in the local directory of priest: "Smith is dead. Don't call him." And "Don't worry if you can't get a substitute for one of the chalicers. We can use one of the canons. That way we can get some work out of them."

Regarding a burial: "Get this—a woman says she outlived two husbands, and, well, they were both jealous, so when she dies she's going to split her ashes in half, some for each."

Regarding a funeral: "On the thirtieth is the funeral of Mrs. X. No, not that Mrs. X—it's the dead one."

When asked what a woman with kids will do without child care during a big service: "Well, she should have thought of that years ago."

Regarding the Choir of Men and Boys: "If the choir men complain about the food provided at Palm Sunday and Easter, send them over to see what the ushers get." And "You said the men of the choir will do anything for money?? We just need them to sing."

After a long discussion about meddlesome choir parents: "I tell you, when I open my church, the choir is going to have nothing but orphans. What an opportunity we had with the German Orphans Home—multicultural singers with no parents."

On state funerals: "We like people to remember the service, not how long it was."

About an ordination service: "The twelve deacons to be made priests need to be taken to the woodshed and told it is not a coronation. This isn't about you, it's about God."

And my very favorite: "The deceased comes highly recommended by the development office."

ON TOP OF THE WORLD

I have thirty-eight years of kids from youth groups and chaplaincy who call to see if I'll officiate at their weddings. For a while I was averaging about fifteen a year. One student said he wanted to know what my stats of successful marriages were before he'd ask me. Ann Selinger and I went back over the records and tried to find out. If the average divorce rate is one out of every two, I'm way, way above average. *So there*, Evan!

There are canon laws that require premarital meetings. It's great to meet with the young people and hear stories of how their romance began and how the groom (and in some cases the bride!) got to the point of popping the question.

In one case I was, along with great friends, a conspirator with the groom.

James Leslie Miles Fisher, a former student, is an actor and film-maker in Los Angeles. One day he called and asked a favor. He wanted to see if he could propose to his girlfriend, Lucy Blodgett, on the top of Washington National Cathedral and asked if I could help him.

Yikes! That was a tall order—pun intended. Because of 9-11 and then an earthquake that caused structural damage, I knew access to the building, particularly the towers, had become extremely restrictive.

I told him I'd see what I could do. I called Katherine Nassor.

If anyone could arrange this, it would be Katherine. One of the longest-serving employees of the Cathedral Foundation, with an unbelievable institutional memory, Katherine knows the cathedral and its labyrinthian governance structure and rules better than anyone.

Initially she balked. But then she said, "It's so romantic." I had her.

Plus, her husband, Ed, was the carillonneur of the cathedral and his keyboard was in the top of the tower! The only thing was, we had to stay with them (not so romantic). We figured out how, at the special moment, Katherine and I would hide in Ed's office.

We arranged that we would meet the couple at the front doors for a special tour of the cathedral, ending with the bells.

I called James. He went nuts. He was so excited. We all were.

When the day arrived, everything went as planned, except at the moment he asked her, the enormous bells began to ring and he wasn't sure if she heard him!

"Will you marry me?!"

She yelled back, "Yes!"

We peeked out the door of Ed's office with a bottle of champagne we had hidden beforehand. It looked like the news was good!

And then we offered a toast to love, literally and figuratively, on the top of the world.

CATHEDRAL ACOLYTES

I have to say being an acolyte (a church server at the altar) isn't all it's cracked up to be. When I was a kid I served at the altar for Father Foote. During the service you'd have to kneel for endless amounts of time. I fainted a couple of times, but at least I didn't throw up like some kids. Most of the time that was because they had been out too late the night before, having raided their parents' liquor cabinets.

One of my favorite acolyte stories was told to me by Dave and Tom Gardner, former St. Albans students and cofounders of the Motley Fool. As kids, a rivalry after a pick-up football game led to a confrontation with some other acolytes in the sacristy of a church. When a priest opened the door, he found the two boys fending off the others with the processional cross!

But those of us who served in parishes were in the minor leagues compared to the Washington National Cathedral acolytes.

For the select few who are chosen to serve, it means an enormous amount of discipline and training by the cathedral clergy and vergers. The young people are chosen from the ranks of Upper School students from St. Albans and the National Cathedral School for Girls. If you ever have the privilege of watching them in person on a regular Sunday or on television at some national event, their dignity and precision are a sight to behold. It is reminiscent of the Changing of the Guard at Arlington National Cemetery.

Having been under such stress during the service, at some point afterward it is important to find a way to blow off steam. The adults on the staff would head over to the Zebra Room, also known as the "Zeeb," a pizza joint that was on the corner of Newark and Wisconsin Avenues, just a couple of blocks from the cathedral. There they would unwind with a pizza and beer provided by Hal and his staff.

As for the kids, I got a call that in the depths of the cathedral some of the maintenance staff found a room stocked with cigarettes and beer. Curiously, no one seemed to know how any of it got in there. I had my suspicions.

It wasn't the vergers or clergy or choir, because they went to the "Zeeb."

It wasn't the cathedral stone carvers. They had their "nest" on top of the central bell tower, surrounded by tastefully arranged empty bottles of Italian wine.

That left only one group who would quickly disappear after the services and were limber enough to crawl into the space.

I suspected it was the acolytes.

Below is the hilarious description of the room by the man who discovered it, Joe Alonso, the cathedral's head stonemason:

The room is under the Nave on the south side. It's actually part of the Cathedral's foundations, which are massive. At one time you were able to access the space before the Nave was completed and now you have to crawl through a very narrow tunnel. Anyway, in the early '90s I found it and there was a table, couple of chairs, some beer and wine bottles and written in chalk on the wall was "This is where the STA boys and the NCS girls lived in sin, 1957."

I crawled back out and left it alone. It must never be disturbed.

There is a famous story told in Episcopal circles about the late actress Tallulah Bankhead attending the midnight Christmas Eve pageant at St. Mary the Virgin Church in New York City. Apparently, Ms.

Bankhead had had a few cocktails beforehand, and as a young acolyte in his magnificent gold embroidered robes swung the thurible (an incense pot) beside her in the back pew, she quipped, "Darling, I love your dress, but your purse is on fire."

THE STONE CARVERS

One of the great joys of working at the cathedral was getting to know the stone carvers. Many years ago, a wonderful documentary featuring them delighted nationwide audiences. Most at the time were of Italian descent. One particular scene in the movie shows them gathered around a table in the cathedral tower after a long day of work, sharing stories and several bottles of wine while carving the fruit they ate into decorative objects.

Many of the carvings in the cathedral celebrate idiosyncrasies of their colleagues that they alone knew. They often poked fun at the cathedral staff as well. If you take a tour up to the central tower, you can see the empty bottles of wine lining the walls. And if you happen to run into Joe Alonso, he might just share some stories with you.

One of my favorites as told by dean Francis Sayre was about a stone carver who asked if his wife's ashes could be interred in the columbarium. He was told unfortunately not. The columbarium holds the ashes of many prominent Americans, including Helen Keller and Annie Sullivan. Disappointed, the stone carver thanked the dean for his time and walked away. Months later the dean asked him whether he had found a suitable resting place for his wife. He said he had and thanked the dean very much for inquiring.

What the dean did not know was that the stone carver had mixed his wife's ashes in the mortar that holds the limestone walls of the cathedral in place.

THE GROUNDSKEEPERS

Maureen Alonso and Joe Luebke oversaw the cathedral groundskeepers. They along with their hard-working staff had the responsibility of caring for the grounds of the entire Cathedral Close, which included those surrounding all of the Cathedral Schools.

In the center of the campus is the Bishop's Garden, surrounded by a beautiful stone wall. With its lovely pathways, gardens, and enormous center lawn, it offers a wonderful respite for anyone who enters. For little boys, however, it is perfect for hide-and-seek behind and under the boxwoods. It is also perfect as a meeting place for the budding romances of the young people of the Cathedral Schools and the occasional student caught smoking.

Maureen and Joe always met the challenges the young people posed with good nature and a sense of humor. Frederick Law Olmstead would be pleased the gardens remain beautiful and intact thanks to the care of these fine people.

A FIRST FOR ME

In 2013 I officiated at my first same-sex union in the cathedral. Drew Tagliabue called and asked if I would do him the honor of officiating, and of course I enthusiastically said, "Yes!"

In 2012 the Episcopal Church authorized a provisional rite of blessing for same-sex unions. Drew and his now-husband Mark, who have been partners for twenty-one years, waited to marry until 2013, when the Supreme Court overturned a key provision of the Defense of Marriage Act, which defined marriage for federal purposes as being "between one man and one woman," allowing states to not recognize same-sex marriages. The Supreme Court declared the provision unconstitutional.

Drew and I have been friends for many years. His parents, Chan and Paul, are among my closest friends. I had officiated at his sister Emily's wedding to John Rockefeller V in 1996 at St. Columba's. I also knew John and his parents, Jay and Sharon. John and his brothers, Charles and Justin, had all been my students at St. Albans.

The Tagliabues were members of St. Columba's, and Drew and Emily were active participants in the youth group while I was there. We had weekly meetings and sponsored retreats for the kids. This next funny story involves Drew.

The youth group kids, chaperones, and I had been on a beach trip over Memorial Day weekend to Rehoboth Beach, Delaware. We were on our way home when we were caught in one of those horrendous traffic jams that happen on Route 50 between Rehoboth and Washington, DC, on holiday weekends.

We were moving at a snail's pace, or stopped, and people were getting out to stretch and walking beside their cars. Radios were blaring, and it was a rather festive atmosphere. Drew was looking out the window when a man got out of his truck, walked over to the car, and tapped on the window. Drew rolled down his window and the man said, "Quit staring at my girlfriend!" and socked him in the face.

To hear Drew tell the story is a riot because as he explains it, "Under the circumstances, it would not have been the girlfriend I would have been looking at!"

Drew "came out" to his parents in the early '90s. The Tagliabues have been wonderfully supportive parents every step of the way. In 2011 a gift from them established the Tagliabue Initiative for LGBTQ Life at Georgetown University.

Cathedral dean Gary Hall welcomed us and I officiated at the blessing of Drew and Mark's union in Bethlehem Chapel in the Washington National Cathedral on December 21, 2013.

Drew and Mark make their home in New York City, where Drew is the head of PFLAG NYC.

Retirement (Sort Of)

My retirement service was at the Washington National Cathedral, with current students, alumni, friends, and parishioners from many years before in attendance.

After thirty years of teaching, pastoral care, weddings, baptisms, and funerals, I knew it was time to retire. As much as I loved the people in my care, the job had become overwhelming to me. I mentioned earlier in the book I'm not very good at setting boundaries, and I was exhausted.

In my farewell, I quoted the writer Paul Hendrickson, who describes "the glorious as a synthesis of the joyful and the sorrowful." That to me is the message of the cross. That is why the cross as a symbol works for me. I had a front-row seat for both joy and heartbreak in the lives of everyone who invited me into them. My life has been and continues to be a "glorious" one. My ministry continues, but is much more manageable.

I moved to a wonderful old house in the Virginia countryside, Cabbage Hollow, and I spend my time gardening and doing weddings, funerals, and baptisms for former students and their families who track me down. I have a winter "gig" teaching at the Episcopal School of Los Angeles.

Years ago, while still at St. Columba's, I remember reading an article written by my friend James A. "Jim" Baker III while he was Secretary of State under President George H. W. Bush. As he left the White House in his limousine surrounded by his Secret Service detail, he caught a glimpse of the former Secretary of State walking all by himself down the street with no entourage. He reminded himself that would one day be him.

I have been gone from the Cathedral Close long enough now that the new folks at St. Albans and the cathedral don't know who I am. It startled me at first, and I have to confess at times I am wistful for the "good old days."

Walter Thorne, my former student, now studying for the Episcopal priesthood, is fond of my saying, "I used to be somebody."

I guess I still am somebody. Just not in charge anymore—if I ever really was. Thanks be to God.

DeCarlo's

Of course, it was hard for me to leave my friends and colleagues, but I couldn't write about leaving Washington without a tribute to my friends at DeCarlo's Restaurant.

Started by legendary DC restaurateur Lucy DeCarlo, it is an institution in northwest Washington in the neighborhood known as Spring Valley. Over the course of my years in Washington, my friends began to refer to it as my "club," and it certainly was. When I'd walk in the door, even before I'd take my seat my drink would appear on the table. The food is always excellent, and it is well known by folks in DC, many of whom are Washington luminaries. Robert Mueller, Bob Schieffer, and noted Washington pianist John Eaton are regulars. There is a salad named for Diane Rehm.

You can't walk through DeCarlo's without seeing old friends and neighbors. The genius of the place is hospitality. The Reverend Steve Huber says he learned everything he needed to know about being a priest after working for Ella Brennan at Commander's Palace in New Orleans. The late theologian Henri Nouwen often spoke of hospitality in his books on living life as a Christian.

More and more young people have discovered DeCarlo's. We laugh that they bring down the median age by about forty years. Now when I go I always take my godson Ed and his sister Elly, who laughingly recall going there with their late grandmother Ellen, who, of course, Lucy would remember. They wouldn't miss it.

RISE, TAKE UP YOUR BED, AND WALK

I had just moved into Cabbage Hollow and I needed a bed. I had noticed an antiques store in a big red barn on Route 29, just north of Ruckersville, and thought maybe they would have something appropriate for a house almost two hundred years old, and they did—a four-poster! It was missing a couple of slats to hold the mattress, but that would be easy enough to remedy. Luckily, I had my friend Doug Shoemaker with me and he could help me carry the pieces to the car.

There was a man sitting behind the desk. I explained I thought I'd like to buy the bed and wanted to know how much they were asking. The man said he would find out if he could. He apologized and explained he was only helping out because the owner was in the back with her husband, who was dying.

After the initial shock of hearing that, I told him I was an Episcopal priest and asked if I could be of any help. He said he would find out. He left and came back a few moments later, saying the owner and her son would like that very much. I followed him through a storeroom into a bedroom in the back. There on the bed lay the man clearly near the point of death. The wife and son introduced themselves and told me how grateful they were to see me.

Luckily, having been at the bedside of many people in the last stages of death, I knew the appropriate prayers by heart and said them. When I was finished, the wife and son thanked me very much and I went back out to find Doug. After a minute, the man who was helping came out and told me the price of the bed. I gave him my credit card, he ran it through the machine, and Doug and I carried the bed out to the car and went home.

The mother and son now have a store in the nearby town of Gordonsville. I shop there from time to time. We really have never spoken of it since, but I can tell they are grateful. It's a beautiful bed. I'm not sure, but I think I may have gotten a discount.

JOHN AND JOHNNY

I tell this story of my neighbors and friends John and Johnny because I found them to be very honest about their sexual orientation at a time when that was difficult in America. Proud of their heritage and of being

American, they both served their country with distinction. They are legends among the folks in Orange County, Virginia.

At the time of his death from heart failure in January 2009 at ninety-one, Johnny Scott was the oldest living descendant of James Madison. He was living with John Trimmer, his life partner of more than forty years, at their farm, Beaumont, on Route 231 in Somerset, Virginia.

John and Johnny both grew up in aristocratic southern families on historic Virginia farms—Johnny at Beaumont, a Madison family farm. The house, a square brick Georgian, served as a hospital during the Civil War. John was raised at Hare Forest, thought to be the first brick home in Virginia in the Federal style. It is believed by many to be the birthplace of Zachary Taylor, the twelfth president of the United States. They met as children; Johnny was friends with John's older siblings. Both attended the University of Virginia.

During the Second World War, Johnny was a sergeant in the army, leading troops in the South Pacific and occupation forces in Japan. He was a decorated officer. John became a navy pilot, flying combat missions in Europe and the South Pacific. After the war, now both openly gay, they eventually returned to Virginia—Johnny to Richmond and John to Orange County.

Fun-loving, flamboyant, and always the life of the party, Johnny often traveled to New York City to stay with his friend the playwright Noel Coward. One night while his host was away, the bedroom door opened and the light switched on. The actress Tallulah Bankhead took one wide-eyed look at Johnny in Noel's bed and exclaimed, "Who the hell are you?!"

Receiving a warning there were to be arrests made of suspected homosexuals in Richmond, Johnny returned to Beaumont in the middle of the night and lived there for the remainder of his life.

Becoming reacquainted with John, Johnny settled down. Understated, quiet, and elegant, John in many ways was Johnny's alter ego.

John moved into Beaumont with Johnny, and they lived with their dog, Gelsimina, while managing the farm. John was for years the business manager of a private school in the Blue Ridge Mountains. They traveled extensively and led very active lives.

Beaumont was the scene of many grand events. Their champagne brunch on Christmas Day was not to be missed. Movies have been filmed there because of the home's historic significance and beauty. Johnny was particularly thrilled to play an extra in them.

For their entire lives as a couple, John and Johnny were embraced by the Virginia communities of Somerset, Gordonsville, and Orange. Route 231, rolling and wooded, is also known as the Blue Ridge Turnpike and has some of the most beautiful farms in Virginia. John recently said that Route 231 was the only place he and Johnny never, ever experienced any kind of discrimination. Sadly, Johnny did not live to see the Episcopal Church's acceptance, or the United States government's legalization, of same-sex marriage.

After Johnny died, John moved into the city of Charlottesville, where he still lives. He said, "It was just too lonely and quiet at Beaumont without Johnny."

Upon his death, many Madison family artifacts at Beaumont were bequeathed to Montpelier, the home of James and Dolley Madison, which had been left to the Trust for Historic Preservation by their friend Marion DuPont Scott. Beaumont now belongs to Ann Thornton, Johnny's niece, who is devoted to John.

When I moved to my home, Cabbage Hollow, in Barboursville in 2000, the folks along Route 231 befriended me. I am fortunate to be a "resident chaplain" to that gang. It was my honor to officiate at Johnny's funeral at Beaumont. It was attended by several hundred people who, in the summer just one year before, had watched Johnny dance the night away at his ninetieth birthday party.

That January, on what was reportedly the coldest day of the year, we bundled up and went out to the pasture. There, surrounded by the cows who joined us to pay their respects, we buried his ashes next to the grave of Civil War soldier Mr. Smith from Alabama, who many years before was embraced by the Madison family and the folks on Route 231.

We then retired inside Beaumont for, of course, a champagne reception.

WATER AEROBICS

Trying to stay in shape at the suggestion of my cardiologist, I joined a water aerobics swim class at our local fitness center, ACAC, in Charlottesville. I had been a jogger for thirty years. When the back and knees began to suffer from the years of pounding on the towpath in DC, I graduated to the elliptical machines at the gym along with swimming. It's much easier on the joints.

It took a bit of courage to join the 6:00 a.m. water aerobics class, as it is dominated by middle-aged women, but one Saturday morning it was led by a man about my age and circumference and I decided to give it a shot. Now I go at least three days a week. We all wear belts that keep us upright in the water. It's probably a good thing there are no underwater cameras filming how adept we are at any of the routines in which we are led. I have a lot more respect for Esther Williams now and am totally convinced synchronized swimming deserves its standing as an Olympic sport.

Just last week I asked Terry, one of my fellow swimmers, if she ever would have imagined we would be "mountain climbing" through the pool to the Eagles 1972 hit "Take It Easy" or to AC/DC's "You Shook Me All Night Long." It seems it was only yesterday I was listening to those songs flying down Three Oaks Road in Jeff Johnson's 1965 Volkswagen Beetle on the way to a party at Cindy Homola's when her parents were out of town. And to think smoking pot is now legal and great for glaucoma and arthritis!

AFTER THIRTY YEARS

Many of my close friends with whom I went to seminary are now of retirement age. I recently was asked to preach at a service at the retirement of the Reverend William Hague, Christ Church Kensington, Maryland, formerly an assistant at Christ Church Georgetown. If you're lucky, a church will get a rector like Bill.

Hello again, everyone. I say again because some of you older lions of the parish might recall I preached at the beginning of his tenure—and now here we are at the end.

I remember years ago in the Diocese of Washington, where there was a lot of enthusiasm, let's just say, about "certain" parishes, and someone would mention Christ Church Kensington—and you'd hear, "Where is that?"

Answer, "Oh, out there somewhere—Connecticut Avenue—beyond the Beltway." Well, those days are gone. You have one of the great parishes in the diocese, and sitting right there is the reason for it. Oh, I know all of you are also the reason, but let's just let Bill have his day.

It is serendipitous that one of the lessons in the lectionary today is the lesson of the Good Shepherd, in which Jesus states, "I know my own and my own know me." It's the key to a great parish—and in Bill Hague you had a good shepherd. I know parts of the service today are taken from the prayer book service called "The Ending of a Pastoral Relationship," which to me is such a downer. So I thought—in the midst of admitting sadness, depression, denial, anger, and existential crush, we ought to have some fun. And remember why we love Bill. And I've had some help from those out there who shall remain nameless, because they prefer I take the hit!

When I first met Bill, I was the only person sitting in the Scott Lounge of the Virginia Seminary. It's an enormous room filled with couches, fifty chairs, and portraits of the deans, and I was way over in a corner in a chair reading. And this person (who may or may not have had an umbrella in his hand due to the threat of rain) walked up to me and said, "Excuse me, but you're sitting in my chair." Now, that was a hint of what was to come.

Another story involved a social group that evolved of which we were a part called the Seminary Gun Club. It had nothing to do with guns. It had more to do with friendship—and bourbon. And one evening, Annilee Brown, the hostess of the Seminary Guest House, was telling a story about a friend who used to twirl her hair when she was nervous. One day as she was twirling, a clump of her hair came out in her hand and left a hole in her scalp. And Bill said, "Well, everybody needs something to pull . . ."

You know, I'm trying to get to the compassionate side of Bill—doing anything to make us feel better.

As in the time he went to see a parishioner who, sadly, had had to have a foot amputated. Bill ended the conversation by saying, "Just put your best foot forward!"

Or when another parishioner called to say her husband, Pete, had just died. Bill said, "Well, for Pete's sake!"

As compassionate, and sweet, and loving as we know him to be, he has made mistakes in his life.

He sometimes misreads things—as the time he was passing by a Martinizing dry cleaner and said, "Oh, look! A one-hour martini zing while you wait!"

And he sometimes, not often, makes mistakes when under pressure, as in his final exam in naval navigation. He plotted a ship from Oakland overland to Chicago—when he was instructed to plot a course from Oakland to Japan.

Also, while in the navy, he was in charge of taking sailors on historical tours of the ports in which they had stopped. Most sailors really had other things on their minds, so he had few takers. The captain decided that the Bill Hague Tour was an excellent chance to punish sailors who had misbehaved, so it became compulsory if the sailors wanted to get out of jail.

Finally, I have to say as much as he loves all of you, he adores his family—and wouldn't you know Bill, not being himself an athlete, marries an award-winning female athlete from Georgetown with a trophy to prove it. (Jane's mother called this the sweaty man award— God rest Ann's soul.) And they have two boys who are athletes. Bill is their biggest fan. The learning curve is a little high.

I knew this in seminary when he asked what a touchdown was, and when at one of the boy's first football games, he thought the game was over after the first quarter and tried to walk on the field to get to his car more quickly. Also, at a soccer game, he dressed in a summer suit, wore a straw boater, brought a picnic hamper full of tea and cookies, and played "Go Fish" with the young siblings of the players.

Truth be told, along with those things about Bill that delight us, you, Christ Church Kensington, have had not just a good shepherd, but a great shepherd. A joyful, brilliant, sweet, kind, gentle, self-

effacing leader. One who at this point in his life can say, "I have known my own and my own have known me."

He has married you, buried you, baptized you, confirmed you, and brought you all into a deeper relationship with God and with one another. It was what he was called to do—there is no question in the diocese where Christ Church Kensington is anymore.

Bill, please stand. You've done your job. "Well done, good and faithful servant."

Jane, J. D., Chris, please stand. He couldn't have done it without you.

And because he couldn't have done it without everyone in this congregation, will you all please stand and let's hear an ovation that the angels in Heaven will hear.

Amen.

RETIREMENT REFLECTIONS

After thirty-plus years of doing church by the book, stepping away has given me a new perspective and I am much more skeptical and honest about rites, rituals, and liturgies that don't seem to work for me anymore. And I am not alone.

I have to be grateful because without church and my religious education, I would never have known about Jesus, but the truth is many clergy friends recently retired feel as I do. The Reverend Barbara Brown Taylor's recent book *Leaving Church* beautifully chronicles her wrestling with such issues, and I have recommended it to many people, lay and ordained, who find themselves in the same place.

For example, I wrote in an earlier chapter the recitation frequently used after a reading is "the word of the Lord" and somebody called out, "Probably not!" Funny as it is, congregations are often not let in on the secret. One of the most egregious examples of this is the citation on the posters you see held up at basketball games, John 3:16 (I am the way, the truth, and the life). If you're lucky enough to be in a congregation that will tell you the truth, you understand that the Gospel of John was written many years after the historical Jesus and the writer of the Gospel only attributed it to him some one hundred years later.

There is a fascinating and controversial group of biblical scholars known as the Jesus Seminar. When they meet as a body, they vote on what are likely the real sayings of the historical Jesus. Fortunately the heart of Jesus comes through loud and clear, though they dispel many myths about the man. In a recent talk I gave on scriptural honesty at All Saints Episcopal Church in Beverly Hills, a young person raised his hand and said, "This makes Jesus much more interesting and *believable*."

PARISH PROBLEMS

At this point in my life, I am just trying to be grateful for having worked in the places I have and for the people for whom I worked. I've been lucky.

In recent years I have become aware of several congregations whose attendance has taken a nosedive because the search committees haven't chosen their rector wisely. It is not for lack of trying. What seems to be occurring is when the new rector arrives, he or she takes little time to really get to know the parishioners. Oftentimes they come with a preset agenda and get extremely defensive when legitimate issues arise. A parish in Washington that at one point had the largest Sunday attendance lost 60 percent of its parishioners and income during the "new" rector's tenure. When the vestry finally acted, it was too late. Many who had once been loyal parishioners found new parish homes or became so disillusioned they quit going to church altogether.

Unfortunately, the only advice I have is for search committees to really do their homework when investigating potential rectors. Find out why the rector will consider moving. References that want to get rid of someone don't always tell the truth for fear the rector won't be called away! Best advice: Go after someone who is happy and successful where he or she is and who turns you down when you first come calling.

PETS

I've suddenly realized that any memoir of mine would be incomplete if I didn't talk about my pets. As a child, Maggie Swift, our black Lab, would grab me by the seat of my pants if I wandered too close to the road. Since then I've had a love affair with all of them: Sassy, Peg, Bingo, Pixie, Nutty, Toby, Popcorn, King, Scruffy, Mebane, and now Jack, for whom I dog-sit. Always unconditionally loving, they have been my best friends, confidants, and confessors. Craig Eder called them "God's messengers from the animal kingdom."

My sisters and I share one big thing in common: We have a terrible time with movies and books about pets. We won't go see the movie or read the book if an animal dies. I think that happened after we saw *Old Yeller* as kids. A few years ago, I mistakenly listened to *Where the Red Fern Grows* on a CD while driving back from Maine. I don't remember driving on the New Jersey turnpike. I sobbed the whole way.

I had to put Mebane down most recently when together we returned from California. He was seventeen. I knew one thing: I wanted to bring him home to Cabbage Hollow to die. We drove almost straight through to Virginia, sharing McDonald's plain cheeseburgers the whole way. My friend Flossie would tease me about getting a hamburger for the dog. I asked one of the attendants at the drive-through if it was unusual for someone to get a burger for the dog. She said, "Everyone does it!"

Though he was partially blind and could barely walk, when we got to the top of the drive at Cabbage Hollow, Mebane turned circles in the back of the car. He knew he was home. He is buried on the hillside where he loved to lie between the pasture and the house.

When I got Mebane, he had been given up by his owner. I didn't ever want him to think I would ever leave him. Luckily, I didn't have to.

When an old friend from Inverness, Jean, died, folks found it difficult to find nice things to say about her, as she had been an alcoholic and had multiple marriages. Mom said of Jean, "Well, she loved kids and dogs."

Not a bad epitaph.

PETS IN CHURCH

It is not all that unusual to have animals in church; for example, on St. Francis Day for the Blessing of the Animals or Christmas Eve pageants. The folks at St. Columba's never got over the time the donkey relieved itself in the middle of the pageant.

Craig Eder's dogs were regulars during children's sermons. Truth is, if you want to captivate children, bring a pet.

The first wedding I had a dog in attendance was Ana Gasteyer and Charlie McKittrick's wedding in New Mexico. Ana was one of the stars of *Saturday Night Live* and has since appeared on Broadway as Elphaba in *Wicked*. She and Charlie had known each other since high school in DC and became reacquainted while both were working in New York City. Ana's parents had moved to Corrales, and Charlie and Ana decided to have the wedding there.

Many couples view their pets as their first child, and being a pet-lover myself, I welcomed their precious Henry, who took part in the procession. Right at the time the congregation is asked if they affirm the marriage with a resounding "We do!" Henry joined in with a great big "Woof!"

Since then I have welcomed many pets, the most recent being Sophie Massey's wedding to Charlie Alvis, where their beloved Zeus lay on Sophie's train between them during their vows.

The only unfortunate incident was when John Brown and Susan Fallon married and their retired therapy dog, Beauregard, had uncontrollable gas in the second pew. John's sister Catherine, who was holding his leash, couldn't stop laughing. People mistakenly thought she was weeping for joy!

Welcome to LA

As it turns out, retirement didn't last very long. I was into my second year when the Reverend Maryetta Anschutz called because she needed my help. I know her to be visionary. A former associate dean at Berkeley Divinity School at Yale and a fourth-generation Episcopal priest, Maryetta recognized the need for a school whose student body would reflect "the vibrant diversity of Los Angeles racially and economically." She is the founding head of the Episcopal School of Los Angeles (ES-LA).

Maryetta asked if I might consider coming to be the assistant chaplain. Because of my not wanting to be away from home, Cabbage Hollow, for an entire year, we agreed I would come and teach during their winter term. I was to help their chaplain, Megan Holloway, as she established her teaching and social service programs. Since then they have invited me back every year, and I've enjoyed keeping my hand in the game.

After the remarkable beauty of the Washington Cathedral Close, ES-LA's neighborhood is a bit of a contrast. Hollywood today is not what those of us who remember the glamour Lucy and Ethel experienced on their adventure there. Even though ES-LA is just a few blocks from Hollywood Boulevard and the stars on the Walk of Fame, the neighborhood was for many years in decline, but no longer. The school now owns two renovated buildings in the heart of Hollywood on the corner of Santa Monica and Lillian Way. The original schoolhouse had once been a post-production studio of Victor Fleming, who directed *Gone With the Wind* and *The Wizard of Oz*. The school's location provides easy access for those who might depend on public transportation. The children come from thirty-seven zip codes.

Thirty percent of the student body is on full scholarship, and another 40 percent on substantial aid. Remarkably, the 30 percent who pay full tuition do not subsidize those on scholarship.

Parents, regardless of their economic situation, are devoted to the mission of the school. They want their children understanding the world as it really is.

The brilliant and creative faculty reflects that diversity as well, and they have come from the finest colleges and universities.

ALL SAINTS EPISCOPAL CHURCH, BEVERLY HILLS

My good friend Steve Huber, formerly vicar of the National Cathedral, is now the rector of All Saints Episcopal Church in Beverly Hills, California. I lived in his guest house while working at ES-LA for the winter. There is a swimming pool between the main house and mine. It's not a bad winter gig.

Steve is a wonderful person with a hilarious sense of humor. We worked together for many years while I was at St. Albans. He is compassionate and an enormously gifted speaker and fundraiser. Before he was a clergyman, he was the head of development for the Human Rights Campaign.

All Saints is one of the most dynamic and creative Episcopal parishes in the nation. It sits on the corner of Santa Monica Boulevard and Camden Drive in the middle of Beverly Hills. They have three services on Sunday along with several during the week. The music program is outstanding, and the choir, led by composer Craig Phillips, is exceptional. Along with an active youth program, they also have any number of outreach programs to the city of Los Angeles and beyond. The living room of the guesthouse in which I stay is currently being stocked with medical supplies that parishioners will take to Honduras. The generosity of the parishioners is unparalleled.

On any given Sunday, you'll see many Broadway, movie, and television stars at All Saints. Sam Waterston, Hal Holbrook, Armie Hammer, Lisa Vanderpump, Carol Potter, and Rod Stewart, along with well-known character actors Chris Ellis and Ray Baker, attend. Over the years many actors were married here, as well as having their children baptized. Funeral services were held here for Humphrey Bogart, Dixie Carter, Anne Jeffreys, and the famed producer Richard Zanuck.

Holidays at All Saints are not to be missed. Of course, people are there for the right reason and worship is beautiful, but probably due the glamour of Hollywood, when it comes time to go up for Communion in the center aisle, you would think you're in a fashion show in Paris or Milan.

Christmas Eve gets more colorful as the evening goes on. At the 11:00 p.m. service, it is not unusual to have a rhinestone-collared Pomeranian carried to the altar rail for a blessing. Southern California weather doesn't usually allow for mink coats, but Christmas is an exception regardless of the temperature. And in Beverly Hills, both men and women love their furs. One regular always wears a large diamond brooch on his coat over a terrific red-silk pajama outfit. Several years ago, the double Communion line slowed to one lane when there was a wine spill because a woman's unusually large-brimmed hat knocked the chalice out of the Eucharistic minister's hands.

Despite the success of many of its parishioners, those in the entertainment industry learn there can be long periods of unemployment. It can lead to loneliness and isolation, and the great success of All Saints is the wonderful and loving community people find in the world that is Los Angeles.

As part of the outreach to the community, the guesthouse is a temporary home to young people, aspiring writers and actors, and many who have come to teach at ES-LA. There is one old person in there too. That would be me.

FAMOUS AND HOMELESS

Francine Dancer is a legend in Los Angeles. I first met her when I opened the garage door at the rectory at All Saints Episcopal Church, upon which she was leaning, and bumped her into the alley. I tried to apologize, but she wouldn't look at me. Francine is homeless.

With the help of Colleen Dodson-Baker, a vestry member and regular volunteer at All Saints, I was able to arrange to apologize to Francine at the church's Monday lunch for the homeless. The luncheon regularly serves approximately one hundred guests and is staffed by volunteers.

Having just applied pink nail polish to her fingernails, she was sitting waiting for me as I walked out of the rectory. A pink flower clip held her shoulder-length blonde hair back from her face. She had on pretty gold earrings.

I asked, "Are you Francine?" After she acknowledged she was, she then said, "I understand you would like to speak with me." I said, "That is true, and I wanted to apologize for bumping you with the garage door." She said she "didn't even remember it."

The first thing she asked me was, "What star sign are you?" I told her Pisces. She said, "I love people who are Pisces. A drag queen in West Hollywood who was a Pisces gave me flowers on Valentine's Day. I love drag queens! They're so sweet and wear such colorful things. Shall we find somewhere to talk?"

Just as we found a place to sit and chat, the volunteer musicians began to play "Proud Mary." Francine immediately whirled around and joined in the singing. "Proud Mary" was followed by "Bring It on Home to Me," "Never Been to Heaven," and "Goin' to Kansas City," at which point she got up to dance with some difficulty due to what she believes is arthritis in her hip. The musicians ended with the gospel favorite "Down to the River to Pray."

She knew every word by heart.

Francine is originally from Kentucky, but has family in Wisconsin. She has one brother still living and several nieces and nephews. As a child, she said she was thought to be dumb. Her mother told her she was crazy. She now believes her learning problems were a result of her having dyslexia. She gets letters and numbers backward. She was "good in art" and "did fine in math until it came time to do algebra."

I told her I identified with that.

She pursued a career as a go-go dancer in Chicago and arrived in LA on a bus in 1979. As a "bikini dancer" in LA, she drew the line when it came to performing in the nude. In the early '90s she met Elton and Betty White, two performers from Arkansas who came to LA to find fame and fortune after a tape of them performing appeared on *The*

Arsenio Hall Show. For a time they had their own cable show in LA, *Elton and Betty White Time.* They encouraged Francine to create her own show, which she did. It was called *The Francine Dancer Variety Show.*

Over the course of her time in LA, she told me she had met Charlie Pride, Wolfman Jack, Debbie Harry, and Zsa Zsa Gabor.

"One time someone called me an icon, but I'm not sure what that is," she said. I told her I thought they meant that as a good thing. She then said, "I'm all over the internet and on YouTube!" That is true. She was also profiled in the April 2006 edition of *LA Weekly.*

When I asked how she ended up homeless, Francine explained, "I had the top-rated public access show in LA for thirteen years, and then one month the check didn't come. I couldn't pay my rent, and I was out on the street."

She receives Social Security, but that only gets her a hotel room for five nights at the beginning of the month. Otherwise, she has a covered spot at a bus stop in West Hollywood unless the police move her along. She keeps some of her belongings in a storage facility in Hollywood.

She carries in her purse an envelope that, she said, contains a ballot on which she voted for Hillary Clinton. She didn't mail it because she didn't have a stamp, but was delighted that "Hillary asked me for five dollars!"

Surrounded by many luncheon attendees, I asked her to describe her life as a homeless person. She looked around at the guests at the luncheon and said, "It's a watercolor painting in the rain."

When she found out I was writing a book, she asked, "Am I going to be in it?"

I said, "Only if it's OK with you."

She said, "Yes, it is."

Then she asked me the title. I told her I didn't have one yet.

She suggested, "How about *Homeless and Famous?*"

She asked me not to reveal her age.

Francine believes in God. She is skeptical of some of the miracles like Jesus walking on the water and the virgin birth, but one night she was being attacked and when she screamed "Jesus!" the attacker stopped. That convinced her. Still, she fears for her safety. She is well acquainted with the other folks living on the street.

Francine finds it very curious that humans are the only creatures who seem to need so much and cannot exist without a roof over their heads. "Gorillas can live in the trees of the forest and birds can make nests out of my hair, but it's funny we can't seem to do it."

I am reminded of Jesus saying in Matthew 8:20: "Foxes have holes, and birds of the air have their nests, but the Son of Man has nowhere to lay his head."

GINO

Gino is in a bad mood this morning, and it's because he had to lock up the church last night and there was a wedding reception. It went 'til eleven o'clock, long past his bedtime. He has been on the maintenance staff for twenty-plus years and is totally reliable. He avoids talk of his past, except for revealing to me that he was once a bouncer at a club on Santa Monica Boulevard and Francine Dancer used to perform there. He said, "She was good!" Legend has it that as a young man he was a professional soccer player.

Because it seemed he had no permanent home, he now lives in a suite in the guesthouse at the rectory, which is known as "The Bishop's Suite," but as far back as anyone can remember, the bishop has never stayed there. The only one who has use of it now is Gino. He is the most loyal of employees.

Last year, when it was discovered someone had made several late-night attempts to break into the church, Gino stayed up all night for several days hiding in the alley behind the church and caught them in the act.

Maintenance staff in parishes see everything. If you ask Gino how things are going in the parish, he says, "They are all cuckoo people." He will do anything for anybody but never first without a question as to why it needs to be done. He calls Hermann, the head of maintenance at All Saints, who is half his size and half his age, "the little boy."

He particularly loves Steve Huber, the rector. This morning while still in his bad mood, I told him Steve was having the vestry over for dinner. He asked, "Who's that?" I answered "the important people." He said, "There is only one important person. That is Steve. The rest of them are dumbsh*ts!

Everyone adores him.

THE CHAMPAGNE MUSIC MAKERS

Last Wednesday night, I gave an opening prayer at a "celebration of life" for Herb Gronauer at 360 North, an old-fashioned, dark-paneled bar and supper club on Palm Canyon Drive in Palm Springs, California. A number of the guests were musical performers who appeared on *The Lawrence Welk Show*, which I used to watch with my folks every Saturday night in the '60s and '70s. I sat next to a member of the Diamonds singing group. One of their smash hits was "Little Darlin'." Across from us sat a member of the Four Lads. One of their big hits was "Moments to Remember."

Herb; his wife, Natalie; and their children, Steve, Vicki, and Julie, were our next-door neighbors in Trout Valley. Herb was a talent agent and a partner in Beacon Artists in Chicago. *Billboard* magazine named him Agent of the Year two years in a row. He represented many of the big acts that came to Chicago: Bob Hope, the McGuire Sisters, Woody Herman, Peter Nero, Red Skelton, the Oakridge Boys, and Tammy Wynette, to name a few. One of his proudest moments was when he booked Frank Sinatra with Count Basie. He would often take neighborhood friends and kids to shows he booked. Carroll Baker was a good friend. The whole neighborhood was excited when Mamie Van Doren came for cocktails at their house. Herb had an engraved watch given to him by Frank Sinatra Jr. As kids, we thought that was so cool. I still do.

Herb was one of the reasons I pursued a career in musical theater in my youth. He came to all our high school musicals. As a teenager, he sent me to an audition at a summer stock production of *Anything Goes* in Michigan starring Dorothy Lamour and I got the part of the bursar! The only problem was I got homesick and came home.

Herb and Natalie retired to Palm Springs many years ago, where he was a board member of the Palm Springs Walk of Stars. He kept his hand in the business as long as his health allowed. Herb was as funny as can be. One line many of his friends remember was uttered one night while out for cocktails. The waitress asked him what he wanted, and Herb replied, "Well, if I could have what I really want, I'd have a milkshake!"

This coming summer I will be officiating at Herb's burial next to the grave of his son, Steven, at Windridge Cemetery in Cary, Illinois. Steve died as the result of an epileptic seizure at camp when he was sixteen. While hiking alone, he fell face first in several inches of water and drowned.

After Steve's death, Herb had less patience for some of the demands of the entertainers while they were on the road. Once one of them threatened not to perform until a case of Coke was delivered to the dressing room. But Herb realized he had to put up with a certain amount of that to pay the bills. He would meet friends who also had retired from the business for breakfast once a week. They would trade funny stories about the stars with whom they had worked. They considered writing a book with each of them taking a chapter, but unfortunately they never got to it. It would have made quite a book!

Although most of the entertainers on *The Lawrence Welk Show* are now gone, I confess on occasional Saturday nights I still tune in to watch Lawrence, Bobby, Cissy, Norma, Joe, JoAnne, Myron, the Lennon sisters, and the rest of "the Welk family" in reruns on public television.

This week, thanks to Herb and a few of the "Champagne Music Makers" still living, I have a few more wonderful "Moments to Remember."

GOOD MORNING, ES-LA!

As you enter the reception area at ES-LA, at its center is a piano on a stage. This particular morning, Eva is playing a piece by Ravel. It is followed by a selection of others by Bach, Scriabin, Barber, and Mozart.

Eva is but one of the many multitalented students at the Episcopal School of Los Angeles. It is not at all unusual to be greeted like this when you arrive. It might just as easily be Hunter Perrin, a fellow teacher and former guitarist for the John Fogerty band, greeting the children on the front steps playing something by Merle Haggard.

I would sometimes sit at the front desk checking students in. All of the faculty share in this responsibility. We also share curb duty, making sure students get dropped off safely.

In the carpool line, before she goes off to work as a maid at a home in Bel Air, a school mom will drop off her son. She could be followed by a studio executive or a television or movie star dropping off his or her daughter.

Just as Washington, DC's industry is government, the industry here in LA is television and film.

Over the course of my time at St. Albans, several difficult news stories occurred involving parents who were well known. Although we couldn't protect the children and their families from the stories in the press, we could support them by listening and being careful to keep their concerns private. At both St. Albans and ES-LA, members of the press can be there only at the invitation of the head of school, unless, of course, they are parents of children who attend. And those particular parents are especially grateful for and respectful of the school's attention to privacy.

Chapel meets three days a week and the entire school attends. Immediately following, the same space is transformed into a lunchroom. Chapels are similar to those at St. Albans. The children regularly deliver the homilies, framed by prayers from the Book of Common Prayer.

ES-LA inspires in the children a passion for social justice. This year the school will graduate its first senior class. These graduating seniors and the young people who come after them will have seen and experienced the plight of the disadvantaged people of Los Angeles in ways most of us never will. They have walked the streets of skid row, helped them do their laundry, and slept on the roof of a homeless shelter.

Last year Walter Thorne, the assistant chaplain, had the children gather on the roof of the shelter on skid row for Compline, a beautiful service of evening prayer found in the Book of Common Prayer. In between readings, he had the children reflect. After the first reading, he asked them to sit quietly and listen to the sounds of the city. After the second, he asked them to look out over the expanse of the city. After the third, he asked them to stand and look down on the street below. To their shock and horror, they watched as a violent attack occurred right before their eyes.

The children have told me the experience was surreal. Walter called the police. The sirens warned the attackers, and as the children watched, they could see them scatter, leaving a woman lying on the ground. They saw where the attackers hid and watched as the police combed the streets searching for them.

One of the boys who witnessed the attack told of the beauty of the moment of prayer, violated by the event. He said it was like something you'd see on TV. It was a reality he had never before experienced. He spoke of a feeling of helplessness.

Just as he described, every week the beautiful prayers of the Eucharist are violated by reenacting Jesus's crucifixion and death. It takes something like this experience from the rooftop to make it real. Unfortunately, it is a reality with which we all must live, along with the hope of a resurrection.

"So, What Do You Think?"
A Homily at ES-LA, Easter 2016

The following is a recent chapel I gave resulting from a question posed to me by one of the kids at the lunch table:

OK, I've got to tell you all something. The week before break, Tom asked me the great existential question, "So, what do you think?"

"Think about what?" I replied.

"Did it really happen?"

"Did what happen?"

"The resurrection."

Ugh. I think my answer was something like "umm uhh duh" . . . and the truth is, for every fifty people you ask if it really happened, you get fifty different answers.

Curiously, there are people who are Christians who reply "Nope," but they still consider themselves Christians because they follow the teachings of Jesus. For those Christians that say "Yes," they have a myriad of ways to explain how resurrection happens. Then there are those who don't care—they treat the Bible stories as interesting historical literature but not to be taken seriously. They're not necessarily atheists; they might believe in the "spiritual," and the Bible is just another book with valuable lessons from which we might learn. Then there are those who think it's all a bunch of hooey!

I want to warn you that my explanation will fall short because when you're talking about resurrection, you're talking miracle. *And miracles are things that defy rational explanation.*

Jesus said on numerous occasions, "Those who have eyes to see, let them see; those who have ears to hear, let them hear." So perhaps you have to have special eyes and ears to experience the miracles around you. And you know what? I think each one of you has them. I think that's what Jesus spent his life on Earth trying to tell us.

It is possible to look at most anything miraculous and find a rational explanation, but I think many would agree that that work of art is much greater than the sum of its physical parts. Similarly, take the miracle of you. Stand up, Tom. It's possible to just see brown hair, a nose ring, and braces—none of which Tom actually has. But when we really, really look at you with eyes for seeing the miraculous, we experience something very special that we can't put into words because words can't contain the essence of You.

And let's face it: Each of us has eyes to see the miracle sitting next to us.

You get it?

You know—nobody saw it *happen. But there were a lot of eyewitness accounts of resurrection appearances of Jesus in the days following.*

So, did it really happen? Sure—why not?! But, I guess you have to have eyes to see it and believe in things you can't exactly explain— like say love maybe.

Amen.

Wacky Wednesday

Hunter Perrin teaches music. He and his wife, Minnow, whom I have known since she was a little girl, live in LA with their brand-new baby girl, True, and their dog, Wolfy.

Minnow's parents, former Secretary of State James A. Baker III and his wife, Susan, are old friends from my days at St. Columba's in Washington, DC. I first knew Minnow, now an actor, as a little girl sitting at my feet during children's sermons.

Hunter and I are often paired together greeting the carpool in the mornings. Last year we decided to make things more interesting by observing what we called "Wacky Wednesday." We would dress up in costumes and Hunter would accompany us while we sang as the parents dropped off their children. Ty, one of the students, would often join us playing his ukulele.

Our debut was to sing the "Oscar Mayer Wiener Song," which was written by Richard Trentlage. His children were my friends while growing up in Trout Valley and they sang the song in the original commercials. It is one of the most famous jingles ever written. That's probably why we all knew it by heart. Dick also wrote "Oscar Mayer Has a Way with B-O-L-O-G-N-A."

We dressed up in hot dog costumes we ordered online, Walter Thorne fired up the grill in front of the school, and Phil Lydeard, formerly our school chef and now athletic director, made "pigs in a blanket" and handed them out to parents and children as they arrived.

We think the kids thought we were nuts, but the parents loved it. They called for more. Since then we have entertained them with songs with the accompanying costumes, such as "On the Road Again" (cowboy hats), "Feliz Navidad" (sombreros), and the theme from *Batman* (capes).

THE THORNADO

I wrote earlier that I hope my real legacy is to be found in the hearts and minds of the young people I have taught over the years.

As I write this, I am driving from Washington, DC, to LA with Walter Thorne. He is affectionately known by the children at ES-LA as "The Thornado."

He was once my student at St. Albans.

Walter is now on the path to holy orders in the Episcopal Diocese of Los Angeles. His, like mine, has been a circuitous route to getting there, from St. Albans on to college and grad school, although he is luckier. He is far smarter, which will help him immensely, particularly in the classroom with smart kids who will test him. (I think he probably knew how to exegete a passage from the Bible *before* he got to seminary.) He can also teach economics and coach.

Something is drawing him to search for the source of love, and he is finding it in what Desmond Tutu called "the clues given in Jesus."

So together now with his students they will continue on that journey. If I had any influence at all, perhaps it was that he picked up on the joy I have found in the "clues" I have uncovered along the way. The clues to love, found in Jesus, and in the people about whom I have written in this book.

When I learned that ES-LA was just down the road from the Henson Studios, I wanted to see if I could arrange to do a chapel with the Muppets. Unfortunately, rights to the Muppets had been sold to Disney, but thanks to filmmaker Phil Hodges, a friend from Washington formerly with Henson Studios, we were able to build puppets representing the faculty and students of ES-LA. The story was titled "A Day in the Life of a Chaplain" and chronicled a day in the life of Walter.

Hatch, Match, and Dispatch

I HAVE FOUND THE EPISCOPAL BOOK OF COMMON PRAYER OFFERS WON-derful liturgical outlines and content for baptisms, weddings, and funerals. There is considerable flexibility, so clergy and couples can personalize the wedding service. It is important to familiarize yourself with it if for no other reason than to make sure you can live with the promises you will be making. The page citations in this chapter refer to the 1979 Book of Common Prayer published by the Church Hymnal Corporation, New York.

I encourage folks to get their hands on a prayer book or check it out online. If you should happen to "borrow" a prayer book from a pew in the back of the church, this will always secretly please the rector and you can always bring it back. I have included general outlines here in the hopes that folks might find them interesting and helpful.

HATCH
The service of baptism begins on page 299. A general outline includes:

- Opening sentences
- Readings
- Presentation of candidates (whether infants or adults)
- Promises of parents and godparents
- The Baptismal Covenant

A "triple header" baptism NELSON HEAD PHOTOGRAPHY

- The prayers
- The baptism
- Closing prayers and blessing
- Concluding Eucharist (optional)

A lot of people make the mistake of believing baptism is a Christian invention. As far as it relates to us who happen to be Christian, it has its roots in Jewish purification rites. Many religions practice such rituals.

Baptism, as understood by Christians, is an initiation into the Christian faith. Jesus was baptized as an adult by John the Baptist. Some Christians believe it should be an adult decision because historians surmise infant baptism began when infant mortality rates were high and ministers were in short supply. People wanted babies baptized "just in case." To me, that is an unfortunate superstition.

There is also another unfortunate belief out there that claims if children aren't baptized and they die, they won't go to heaven. That does not sound at all like Jesus's view to me. He held children in the highest

"Will, stop!"

regard, saying, "Let the children come to me because to them belongs the kingdom of God."

As for baptizing infants, I took my cue from the late Bishop John Walker. He believed if the Holy Spirit is conferred in baptism, why not begin as early as possible.

We practiced performing baptism with doll babies while in seminary. Episcopalians generally don't dunk. They sprinkle. We had to make sure we didn't drown the baby or drop it. It can be a problem if you have a squirmer.

You also have to be careful not to wait too long. When children get a little older, they often meet baptism with suspicion. A good trick is to sprinkle Mom's and Dad's heads first.

My first memory of performing a real baptism was in Barrington Hills. It was very traditional, as most have been since then, taking place in the church's font or in a parishioner's home. I have had a couple of interesting ones, such as in a birdbath in a garden.

But the one in the ocean could have ended in disaster.

I had been invited by my seminary classmate, the Reverend Gil Birney, to be a summer supply rector at his church, St. Bartholomew's in North Yarmouth, Maine. One of his parishioners requested that their baby's baptism be in the ocean. Gil and I loved the idea. So, we put on our swimsuits and headed out to the beach. He took the first part of the service and then handed the baby off to me for the second half.

As I was walking out into the surf, Gil yelled, "Will, *stop!*"

I was about to walk off a sandbar with the baby in my arms.

While in seminary, my friend JoAnne Thompson witnessed a full immersion baptism at a Baptist church in Alexandria, Virginia. The baptismal pool was in the front of the nave, located high above the choir seats, complete with a painted backdrop featuring palm trees. When the candidate for baptism descended the stairs to the pool, she slipped and fell into the pool, creating a wave that washed over the heads of the choir.

I continue to officiate in calmer waters for the children of my former students.

Recently three best friends from St. Albans, Bill Hughes, Mark Storch, and Jamie Head, asked to have their newborns baptized together in the Bethlehem Chapel in the Washington National Cathedral. They remembered it fondly from their days at St. Albans. It has a beautifully carved marble baptismal font dedicated to Bishop Angus Dunn. Bishop Dunn was a real character. When he would meet with a seminarian he would ask, "Do you know how tough you have to be to be a priest? You have to be this tough." He would then pick up an ice pick he kept on his desk and ram it into his leg. What the seminarian didn't know was that he had a wooden leg.

MATCH

The service for the Celebrating and Blessing of a Marriage begins on page 423 of the Book of Common Prayer. A general outline includes:

- Opening sentences
- The Declaration of Consent
- The Ministry of the Word (readings)
- A homily (if desired)
- The marriage
- The prayers
- The blessing of the marriage
- Concluding Eucharist (optional)

A new liturgy appropriate for same-sex marriages is available. Interestingly, with its new language, it is sometimes preferred by couples of the opposite sex.

Homilies

I work pretty hard on my homilies, and when it comes to speaking in general, I prefer to deliver what the late Reverend Edgar Romig, rector of Church of the Epiphany in Washington, DC, coined a "homilette."

A few years ago, I had a wedding in a historic church in southern Virginia (no AC) in the late summer. I was so hot my glasses steamed up and I couldn't see a thing I had written, so I winged it during the homily.

Afterward, I asked the bride's mother if the homily was OK. She said, "Oh, I don't know . . . I never listen anyway."

After twenty-five years at St. Albans, a lot of my former students ask me to officiate at their weddings. I am flattered at these times, when it's just as easy to ask a close friend who can get "ordained" online. A student once paid for an ordination certificate for me in case I ever happened to get excommunicated. So far, so good.

Lately, since I've "retired" and live in Virginia, it is sometimes hard to get together for a premarital meeting. So in that case I have the couple write to me and tell me some things about themselves and their relationship so I can make the "homilette" more personal. The questions I ask them to answer generally are:

- Let me in on how you met . . . the romantic and fun stuff.
- What are the challenges of maintaining a relationship in the face of educational demands and challenging careers?
- Tell me about your folks' relationship, what you liked and what you'd do differently, because they've been models for you.
- Are there any issues in your families that might pose a challenge in the long term; e.g., difficult people, illness, financial worries?
- Is there anything in particular you are worried about?
- Do you see children in your future?
- And finally, just what is it that holds you two together?
- Discuss where you're coming from religiously, whether you consider yourself religious or not, because I want the service to be true to who you are.

The couple's answers are always thoughtful and reflect the personalities of each person. Their thought processes can be so different. I recently officiated at the wedding of Claire DeBord and Peter Bixler in Greenwich, Connecticut, where I held up the pages of the letters they had written to me—the groom wrote *two* pages, the bride wrote *ten*. I described them as "stream of consciousness meets succinct, or Virginia Woolf meets Ernest Hemingway."

Venues

Honestly, as far as wedding advice goes, it depends totally on the venue. If you're in a church, brides and grooms tend to go with the traditional. I've recently had a lot of weddings outside, and the musical choices are varied. Generally, the couples employ a string quartet or a harpist, which works well.

Outside weddings are very popular, but you have to be mindful of the weather, particularly the bugs and the heat and humidity. There can be mishaps.

When Mary Bruce and Phil Levis married at the Bruce's farm in Virginia, we had to pick a cricket off the bride's veil during the vows.

I officiated at Stephanie Ruhle and Andy Hubbard's wedding several years ago in a beautiful setting in the New Jersey mountains. It was very warm. One of the groomsmen fainted right in the middle of the couple's vows. He was caught in midair by the musicians and carried behind a potted plant that was concealing them. Once we saw the groomsman was OK, Stephanie looked at me and calmly said, "Keep going."

My brother-in-law Larry also fainted at his wedding to my sister Kim. It was a Catholic Mass in an un-air-conditioned church on about the hottest day of the year. The officiant took a bowl of holy water and dumped it over his head. He finished the service sitting in a chair. We weren't sure if the cause was the heat or the rehearsal party the night before. Probably both.

Caution

Be careful with candles, especially when they are placed anywhere on the floor. When Meredith Scott and David Pfeffer married, a young woman wearing a pashmina accidentally dropped one end in a candle set in a hurricane lamp at the end of the pew. When the flames erupted across her back, a young man sitting behind her tackled her to put the fire out.

On another occasion for the same reason, the floor-length dress of the mother of the bride caught fire as she descended down the stairs at the reception. Quick action on the part of one of the guests saved her from injury as well.

My final advice for all older attendees: If you can avoid it, never take a bus to the wedding venue. The bus never leaves when you're ready to go home.

Photographs

Photographs are also to be met with caution. If the bride and groom aren't clear and careful, the wedding can end up looking like a Hollywood photo shoot. If the wedding is in a church, they generally have rules as to

Th bishop and the GoPro

what is and is not allowed. I learned that many years ago at St. Columba's when the videographer popped up behind the altar in full view of the congregation.

It's nice to put what is expected of guests somewhere in the program. Best advice is to see that cell phones are silenced and leave the picture taking to the designated photographer. People taking pictures during the service block the views of those standing or sitting behind them.

One inventive St. Albans alum I recently married in the Little Sanctuary brought a GoPro. We looked around for the most unobtrusive spot to film the ceremony. It ended up being held in the hands of the statue of Bishop Walker. It is a favorite photograph of the Walker family.

Flowers

Most couples are mindful of wedding costs, and because flowers can be expensive, they are generally beautiful and modest. But there have been moments. Several years ago, a couple at St. Columba's had a Hawaiian-theme wedding. They brought in potted palms with pineapples placed in them. A parishioner who entered the church before the wedding quipped, "Who's getting married, Tarzan and Jane?"

Cakes

Anita McManes is a fabulous pastry chef, so when her daughter Linda was to be married, she was very particular about her choice of bakers. Linda's beautiful reception was held in the ballroom at the Cosmos Club in Washington, DC. When Anita arrived at the reception, the cake wasn't at all what she expected. When she later inquired at the bakery, they were shocked by her description of the cake. Upon investigation they learned the driver of the van transporting the cake slammed on his brakes on the way to the reception, smashing the cake. The driver then went to the local Giant, bought two vanilla sheet cakes, rearranged the flowers, and tried to pass it off as the one Anita had chosen. As inventive as he was, he got fired.

John and Emily Rockefeller married on an extremely warm evening. The reception was under a tent at the Rockefellers' estate in Rock Creek Park. I was sitting next to the table displaying the cake. It was multi-tiered, and I noticed one of the tiers beginning to give way. Just as I was about to stick my fingers in the cake to hold it up, a waiter quickly took note and several members of the staff raced over to keep the cake from toppling.

Music

Best advice: Be mindful of appropriate lyrics.

A great friend of mine, an Episcopal bishop, was officiating at the second marriage of a fellow clergyperson. Without her knowledge, the bride had secretly arranged with the organist to sing her favorite song ("Somewhere Over the Rainbow") to the groom immediately following the blessing of the marriage. It was quite a surprise to the attendees.

If you pick a hymn or song for everyone to sing during the service, be sure to choose one with a tune everybody knows, and don't assume everything in the hymnal is appropriate. When an STA alum chose "Lift Every Voice and Sing," a favorite hymn of his and his classmates', he found it probably not suitable because of the lyrics "blood of the slaughtered."

The Reverend Billy Shand reminded me of another one *not* to use: "Hail the conquering hero as he mounts his steed in triumph."

Also, if you're using a DJ, be careful because sometimes when DJs introduce the wedding party, they make them sound like contestants on *The Price Is Right*—"Let's give it up for Karen and Richard! Woohoo! Come on down!"

Readings

As far as readings at weddings go, choose ones that are thoughtful and meaningful to the couple. They don't need to always come from scripture. The prayer book gives you lots of suggestions.

There is the ever-popular "Love is patient and kind . . .," that beautiful passage from Corinthians. Also "Arise, my Love, my fair one, and come away . . ." from the Song of Solomon. The only danger in the latter is if the reader gets nervous and keeps reading beyond what he or she is supposed to, it ends with, "poor little sister hath no breasts, what shall we do with her on the day she is spoken for?" My friend Stewart Bryan used to read that to his sister Flossie and make her cry.

Over the years, I have heard passages from Winnie the Pooh and Dr. Seuss, all charming and perfectly appropriate. Just recently I heard "Falling in Love Is Like Owning a Dog" by Taylor Mali and a passage from the movie *When Harry Met Sally* .

I recently officiated at a wedding where luckily the groom thought twice about reading "You Don't Need a Man, You Need a Goddamn Warrior."

Toasts

Toasts are where you can really get into trouble. I end most wedding rehearsals with the following words of advice to the bridesmaids and groomsmen: "If you've had a couple of drinks at the dinner and you're not sure if your toast is appropriate, it isn't."

Several years ago, I officiated at a wedding and the father of the bride started his toast at the reception by saying, "When Susie was one . . ." Susie was thirty-two years old. He went through every year of her life. You can imagine how long that took.

Weddings, as beautiful as they are, are fraught with perils. I tell couples they have absolutely no control over how anyone is going to behave. Rehearsal dinners and receptions are far more dangerous than the wedding itself—unless, of course, the minister goes rogue in the service and gives a way too long sermon talking about himself or herself or, even worse, the meaning of marriage, because an explanation is to be found within the liturgy itself.

Cocktail Hour

Real mistakes happen when toasts commence after a really long cocktail hour when the bridesmaids and groomsmen are already smashed before they begin. You know you are in trouble when a drunk bridesmaid starts to cry or (even worse) when a groomsmen starts to talk about the night someone vomited.

I've had brides and grooms furious with family members and friends who have given toasts that offend. Here is some advice from experience:

- Don't get drunk.
- Don't talk about how "close" you are to the bride or groom and that you've known him or her longer than anyone else.
- *Never, ever* talk about exes.
- Don't talk about getting drunk or doing drugs.
- Don't talk about trips you have taken together (really boring).
- Don't take your clothes off.
- Don't hand out a list at the rehearsal dinner about who is sharing a room with whom.

In my book, the record set for the most toasts at a wedding stands at forty-two. I had to go home and walk the dog before they were over.

Really Stupid

Several years ago, a friend attended a formal evening wedding in a historic Episcopal church near Charlottesville, Virginia. At the point at which the minister asked the congregation, "If anyone knows any reason the couple should not be married, speak now or forever hold your peace," two women in evening dresses in the back row stood up, stomped their feet, yelled something, and stormed out of the church.

They were actors hired by one of the groomsmen.

A Homily for Karen and Will Cosmas

Karen and Will, it is an honor to be here. Thank you. For those who might not know, I've been a friend of the Cosmases for thirty-some years.

Karen, welcome to the family. Will's father, as you know, is an Emmy Award–winning television producer. No sitcom he ever produced could match the real-life one he had at home. He knew it and loved every minute of it.

Now, bride and groom, you two are well on your way to producing your own show.

To hear of your courtship sounds like a cross between Friends *and* Seinfeld. *We're all part of the cast. Over here you've got the Soup Nazi and Kramer. Over here you've got Elaine. Over there you've got* All in the Family *with Archie and Edith. Sitting right here in the front row from* I Love Lucy *you've got Lucy and Ricky and Ethel and Fred. You get the point?*

And the amazing thing is, there's no script! Every day there's a surprise episode.

C. S. Lewis wrote a book entitled Surprised by Joy.

Karen and Will, in the presence of all the characters in this real-life sitcom, you will reach out and take what and whom you have been given by the grace of God, and today—you win the Emmy.

Amen.

DISPATCH

My will to my Dear Children:

I won't be separated from any of you Dear Children. I'll only be closer to God.
Bury my body as cheaply as you can and forget it.
Think of me as living near and loving you
And knowing more and more the things I want to know
And growing more and more into what God wants me to become.

"They shall not walk in darkness."
Love, Mother

— ZENO OTILLIA "TILLIE" BILLOW (1926)

Several years ago, I found my great-grandmother's will (above) in a family Bible. I frequently quote it at funerals for family and friends. I have reached the stage in my life where I find myself in a conversation with good friends about what they want for a funeral. "Funeral" sounds *so funereal* and "memorial" isn't much better, so most of the time people call the gathering a "Celebration of Life."

The conversations are heartfelt and generally filled with laughter. When speaking of things to include in his obituary, one friend told his family he wanted to include "Price Club" in his list of club memberships. It is an important conversation to have with your loved ones. More often than not, families and friends are caught off-guard when someone dies and they don't have a clue as to the deceased's wishes. "Deceased" is actually another unfortunate word. It ranks right up there with "cremains."

And speaking of cremains (ashes, as they are generally known), it is nice to know where folks would like to be interred or sprinkled. Any number of my friends are still keeping their loved ones on the mantle or on a bookshelf or carrying them around months and even years later. A distant relative of mine who didn't have a particularly happy marriage kept her husband's ashes in the trunk of her car until she decided what to do with them. One funny story involves my friend Jane, who with the help of her children was cleaning out her basement during a move. Her son found a box and asked her what to do with it. She said, "Pitch it. Oh no, wait! It's your father!"

"Will, if anything good comes out of this, I'm giving you all the credit," Frank Fowlkes told me after we said a prayer during the last stages of his illness, meeting the reality of his situation with clarity, hope, and a sense of humor. I have spent many hours with people at the end of their lives, and I am always astounded by their courage.

At such a time, people fall back on tradition. Some folks remember a time when remembrances were only for receptions following a funeral, not to be within the service itself. According to the prayer book, even homilies are optional. Here's some advice on what to do and perhaps what *not* to do.

There are two burial services: Rite One, page 469 (the old-fashioned language that some prefer), and Rite Two, page 491 (which is a little more contemporary). Flip through the pages of the services. It has recommendations for readings among the prayers.

Of course, you can go online and find many different suggestions for orders of service. But here is a workable outline if you're going by the Episcopal book:

- Opening sentences
- A prayer
- A hymn or psalm
- A reading
- A gospel reading
- A homily (optional)
- A Eucharist (optional)
- A confession of sin (optional)
- The Lord's Prayer
- The prayers (a selection from which to choose)
- A final blessing and dismissal (if no body or ashes are present)
- The Commendation (if a body or ashes are present)
- A final hymn or song

A Service of Committal (page 482) happens at the gravesite. Hopefully, one has been chosen. A body is buried. Ashes can be interred, buried, or scattered.

A word of warning: Be careful about eulogies! Two at best, maybe three, and limit them to three minutes. Choose your speakers carefully. They'll probably speak seven minutes, and you'll have added twenty-one minutes to the service. Remember the advice of Bill Peterson, the late Director of Worship at Washington National Cathedral: "You want people to remember how beautiful the service was, not how long it was!"

As far as hymns go, pick your favorites but, again, with a familiar tune people can sing. If you're lucky, as I was, the church musicians will have the pastoral care of parishioners first and foremost in their minds. When it came to funerals, the musicians with whom I worked would always try to accommodate requests, and some of the requests can be unusual, such as:

- "Joy to the World," Three Dog Night version
- "Hail to The Redskins," composed by Barnee Breeskin (lyrics by Corinne Griffith)

- "I Walk the Line," Johnny Cash
- "Lush Life," Nancy Wilson
- "Stars and Stripes," John Phillip Sousa
- Theme from *Star Wars*, John Williams
- "Stairway to Heaven," Led Zeppelin

At least I never had a request for "Ding-Dong! The Witch Is Dead," which was actually banned by a Roman Catholic bishop in Australia because of its popularity.

Buzz Beler, the owner of the Prime Rib in Washington, arranged for the combo from the Prime Rib to play a selection of his favorite songs at his brother's service at Gawler's Funeral Home. The favorite: "My Way."

The Really Unexpected

One of the most emotionally challenging times I ever had was when the father of the groom was killed in an accident the day before his son's wedding. Bravely, the bride and groom decided to go ahead with the wedding. The first of the week, I then officiated at the father's funeral.

Passages

My friend Flossie, originally from Richmond, Virginia, is the daughter of the late David Tennant Bryan, publisher of the *Richmond Times-Dispatch*, and his wife, Mary Davidson Bryan. Flossie moved to Washington, DC, while married to her second husband, Ellis Wisner, a teacher. Together they have a son, Bryan.

Ellis's father, Frank Gardiner Wisner, worked for the CIA. After Mr. Wisner's death, Ellis's mother, Polly, a famous Washington hostess, married the well-known American journalist Clayton Fritchey. They held many events at their home in Georgetown. Polly Fritchey's best friend was Katharine Graham, publisher of the *Washington Post*.

Upon hearing of the death of prominent politician Averell Harriman, Clayton Fritchey asked Flossie, "Are you going to the Harriman funeral?"

Flossie: "No sir, I never met Governor Harriman."

Clayton: "What difference does that make?"

TOO MUCH INFORMATION

While my friend Flossie and I were attending a funeral in Washington National Cathedral, a very prominent and elegant couple walked up the center aisle searching for seats. The wife wore a full-length mink coat. Flossie turned to me and said, "They're nudists, you know."

OH, KATRYNA! REMEMBER WHEN WE WERE RICH?

While chaplain of St. Albans, I met two of the most remarkable women I have ever known: Marie-Dennett McDill and Katryna Carothers. I think it only appropriate that I write about them together, as they were best friends and celebrated residents of Georgetown. The truth is I can't think of one without thinking of the other, and neither can anyone else who knew them. Their sons all attended St. Albans.

One of my first memories of them is the day they invited Flossie Fowlkes and me to tea at the Four Seasons Hotel in Georgetown.

There they were, Marie-Dennett with her flaming red hair and lipstick and the diminutive and elegant Katryna sitting next to each other on a loveseat in the hotel lounge. Early in the conversation the two of them were reminiscing about living in Georgetown with their former husbands when Marie-Dennett said in her mellifluous and whimsical way: "Oh, Katryna! Remember when we were rich?" Then singing, she launched into her rendition of "Three Little Maids" from *The Mikado*, changing the lyric to "Two little maids from Dumbarton Avenue . . ."

Somehow or another, during tea we got on the subject of church . . .

Marie-Dennett: "I *hate* Communion."

Flossie: "I do too!"

Katryna: "But . . . I *love* Communion."

Me: [silence]

Marie-Dennett, a daughter of H. Gabriel Murphy, former owner of the Washington Senators, had grown up on an estate on Chain Bridge Road in Washington, DC. Her mother, the former Marie McIntyre, was a close friend and bridge partner of Mamie Eisenhower's. Mrs. Eisenhower would send her driver to pick up her friends, the reason for that perhaps having had something to do with the cocktails at lunch.

A talented artist and writer, Marie-Dennett attended Visitation Convent School in Washington. Following the wishes of her father, she gave up her dream of attending art school and went on to Manhattanville College. She married Paul Gardner, a lawyer, and lived on Dumbarton Street in Georgetown with their two sons, David and Thomas, and daughter, Mackie.

Katryna was raised in New York, the daughter of Phillip M. and Elizabeth Haskell Brett, and graduated from the Columbia School of Arts and Sciences. She married George Herrick, a diplomat, and after living in Brussels, moved in a few doors down from the Gardners with their three boys, Jason, Timmy, and Adam.

While in Brussels, Katryna suffered a brain aneurysm, which left her partially paralyzed. She had to relearn how to read, talk, and write (using her other hand). An accomplished artist, her paintings are exquisite. She was well known in Georgetown and was frequently spotted driving her specially equipped and brightly decorated golf cart.

While in the fourth grade and jogging on the track at St. Albans, Katryna's son Adam would be stricken with the same type of aneurysm.

The children of both families were and remain close friends to this day. But little did they know *how* close they would become until Katryna and Marie-Dennett decided to divorce their husbands at the same time. In a situation reminiscent of that which Lucille Ball and Vivian Vance might have faced in an episode of *The Lucy Show*, they packed up their six children and moved into the historic schoolhouse on the Murphys' estate until their divorces were finalized.

Not long after our tea, I was invited to dinner at the house Marie-Dennett had purchased post-divorce on 34th Street in Georgetown. Marie-Dennett, not known for her culinary or housekeeping skills, had ordered out. After her death, her son David was quoted in the *New York Times*, saying, "It was not that she *could* not cook. It was that she *did* not."

After cocktails, we helped ourselves to Chinese carry-out. We sat down in the dining room and immediately Katryna, with the one hand she could raise, lifted her linen napkin high above her head and then dropped it on the table and simply said, "Marie-Dennett . . . *wet!*"

Marie-Dennett, who just laughed at her own attempt to iron the napkins, walked over to the fireplace and proceeded to light a fire. Soon after, smoke filled the dining room and then the fire alarm went off.

If you know anything about Georgetown, nothing scares residents more than a fire. Houses are closely attached, and the narrow streets and parking make it very difficult for fire trucks to get through. I ran to the basement to find the reset button, but it was too late. The fire department was on its way.

Soon the street was blocked at both ends by an array of fire trucks. When the fire chief arrived, somebody sent him down to the basement, where I remained with my finger on the alarm button to keep it from ringing. When the smoke cleared and the alarm stopped, I came back upstairs. The chief looked at me disdainfully and said, "Next time, Mr. Gardner, check the damper before you light a fire." Offering no explanation, I said, "Yes sir, I will."

Eventually Katryna and Marie-Dennett were to meet the men who would become their second husbands.

Marie-Dennett sold the house in Georgetown and moved to South Woodstock, Vermont, into the "Owen Moon House." A former residential school converted into a home, there Marie-Dennett could have her own art studio. A most remarkable thing about the property was that it had its own stone amphitheater, where she hosted dinner parties—catered, of course.

While in Woodstock, Marie-Dennett met and married Jonathan McDill, who had formerly been the librarian of Dartmouth College. Katryna married Neil Carothers, a career diplomat, and continued to live in Georgetown. I had the privilege of co-officiating at both of their second weddings . . . and the funerals of their husbands.

Sadly then, their own funerals were to follow.

Katryna died of ovarian cancer on July 4, 2007. She faced her illness with her characteristic gentleness, elegance, and dignity. We interred her ashes next to her beloved Neil in the memorial garden at Christ Church Georgetown.

We *did* have Communion.

Marie-Dennett came to the funeral, but she was not her character-istic vibrant self.

Having discovered she had lung cancer, Marie-Dennett put her home in Vermont on the market and took an apartment in the Carlyle Hotel in New York City. The hotel would provide the services she needed, and it was close to Central Park, where she would take frequent walks. It was also central for her children. Thomas and David, as cofounders of the Motley Fool, divided their time between New York and Washington. Daughter Mackie, who bears a striking resemblance to her mother, was an interior designer in Charlemont, Vermont, and made frequent buying trips to the city.

Marie-Dennett's disease progressed rather quickly. At her request and because of my devotion to her, I made frequent trips to New York. She died on October 15, 2008. We had her memorial service at St. Bar-tholomew's Church. A reception followed, with music provided by a jazz ensemble from the Carlyle. News of her death and the style in which she chose to face it made the front page of the October 28, 2008, edition of the *New York Times*.

Her burial was another story . . .

The children couldn't decide where to bury her ashes. She absolutely did *not* want to be buried next to Jonathan in his family plot in Vermont. Several months later, Mackie determined that the only suitable place was George Washington's home, Mount Vernon.

No one really knew what connection Marie-Dennett had with Mount Vernon, but we all went along with Mackie.

So as not to draw attention to ourselves, we all (the entire family, grandchildren included) walked casually through security with her ashes concealed in, according to her daughter Mackie and daughter-in law Margaret, "a brown quilted Chanel tote with a silver metal chain-link shoulder strap." We then strolled through the grounds of Mount Vernon, looking for the perfect place . . .

We found it under an enormous cedar tree at a point overlooking the Potomac River. There, hidden from the tourists by the branches of the tree, we scattered the ashes. The grandchildren spoke, and I read the committal service from the prayer book I had used at Marie-Dennett's wedding to Jonathan.

We did *not* have Communion.

FOR KATRYNA
A Homily Preached at Christ Church, Georgetown,
at the Funeral of Katryna Carothers

Darlington's Fall, *a novel by Brad Leithauser and illustrated by his brother Mark, chronicles the life John Darlington, a young naturalist who, while reaching for the rarest of butterflies, falls from a cliff and is disabled for life.*

Who could have imagined the circumstances in which Katryna found herself after her "fall." We all marveled as she too found herself standing on another shore—her own—after seeing the world with new eyes and new appreciation for life and creation, evident in her attention to detail. Her powers of observation reflected in the way she lived, and through her exquisite art.

Her determination—or sheer grit, as Flossie Fowlkes would describe it—took her beyond where many of us might have ventured. This new shore upon which she stood was what the Bible might call Holy Ground. In all honesty, I have found very few people in this life who find themselves standing there; living so intensely in the presence of God, they have a certain radiance about them. (I think I now understand the story of the transfiguration.) I think you all know of what I speak.

By no means do I mean to imply she was an ascetic. Katryna was too well grounded in the lives of her children, family, and friends to have abandoned us to the mountaintop. But we who were fortunate enough to have known her have, I believe, known someone who the author Marcus Borg would call a "spirit person"—a person for whom God is an experiential reality.

Once we see that in someone, each of us is never the same.

I would like to conclude with an ancient Celtic prayer from Scotland:

I am serene because thou lovest me. Because thou lovest me,
naught can move me from my peace. Because thou lovest me,
I am one to whom all good has come.

Amen

Johnny Apple

In the early morning hours of October 5, 2006, Pie Friendly called and simply said, "Will, Johnny died." Johnny was her brother-in-law, the husband of her sister Betsey.

R. W. Apple Jr.—or "Johnny," as he was known to his friends and colleagues—was for more than forty years a correspondent and editor at the *New York Times*. He was a brilliant and exacting wordsmith who his reporters feared as much as admired. The stories he covered took him to the far reaches of the globe and found him at the center of historic world events. He was even rumored to have told Robert F. Kennedy about the death of Dr. Martin Luther King. But I knew him best as a devoted husband and stepfather.

Johnny and Betsey Apple had been friends of mine for many years. His stepson John had been my student, and I had been the officiant at his wedding to Susan Fallon as well as his sister Catherine's wedding to Grant Collins. John and Catherine were devoted to Johnny and vice versa. Johnny attended many of the children's school and sporting events. He also remained friendly with the children's father, Preston Brown, a lawyer who lived in Washington.

I had known for some time that Johnny was suffering from thoracic cancer. He and Betsey had temporarily moved out of their home in Georgetown and taken a one-floor apartment downtown near the hospital. It was becoming increasingly difficult for Johnny to get around.

We had a very private funeral for him in the Little Sanctuary at St. Albans School, which was attended by family and a few close friends. Johnny grew up a Lutheran. It was a very traditional Episcopal service, and because much of it was written by Thomas Cranmer, we thought

Johnny would approve, as he was an admirer of the great writer. Over the years, Johnny and I had numerous theological discussions. I learned a lot from him. He really was much more a scholar than I. I love it when reporters take on the Gospels and church history with their investigative skills. Having learned in a recent email from him the roots of his religious education in Akron, I was sure to include the great hymn penned by Martin Luther, "A Mighty Fortress."

Another public memorial, the likes of which I have never seen, would be held at the John F. Kennedy Center for the Performing Arts. Throughout his colorful career, and as he traveled the world for the *New York Times*, Johnny had also served as a food and wine critic. After formal tributes from Todd Purdum, Lord David Owen, Senator John McCain, Alice Waters, and Calvin Trillin, the celebration continued. Chefs and winemakers from around the world catered the reception, which was attended by over a thousand people.

In 2009 a collection of Johnny's articles came out in a book appropriately titled *Far Flung and Well Fed: The Food Writing of R. W. Apple.*

This was a spectacular life, but as I conclude this memory of Johnny, I have to confess what I'm really hoping is that I have all the punctuation in the right place.

THE 2 PERCENT FACTOR

One of the most fascinating things I have learned in my life is how brave people are after the shock of the diagnosis and the fight for your life, when you realize you *really are* going to die. The people with whom I have been present at such moments have met it with amazing clarity and resolve.

In his forties, married with two young children, Gary Hayes had been a serious athlete all his life. One morning he came back from a jog on the towpath and got into the shower. When he got out, he looked in the mirror. His skin was yellow.

The diagnosis was advanced pancreatic cancer. Gary and his wife, Susan, were friends socially in Washington. They had two young boys. He grew up as a Roman Catholic, but didn't have much use for the church. He said just because he was dying, he didn't want to be a hypocrite, but in his own words he believed in what he called the "2 percent factor." For Gary, there was a 2 percent chance God existed.

That's where our discussions began, and, frankly, that's exactly where they ended. At his funeral I wanted to respect his view, from which he never wavered. He was a person of great integrity.

And to tell you the truth, a lot of folks feel the same way. The temptation when someone dies is to attribute to them more faith than they actually had.

I hope I will be as honest and brave as the people I have loved who have had to face whatever death means. I do take comfort in biblical metaphor. Having faith the size of a mustard seed seemed to be enough for Jesus.

Which, as far as I'm concerned, comes out at about 2 percent.

INTERFAITH SERVICES

Because the St. Albans community is very diverse, I am asked to officiate at a lot of interdenominational and interfaith services. They can be quite beautiful, but a lot depends on the attitudes of those involved.

One wedding in particular involved a faculty member from St. Albans who was Jewish. His bride was Roman Catholic. The Reverend Claudia Gould and I officiated together, and we tried very hard to be respectful of both traditions. At the reception we were seated at a table with a Roman Catholic couple and a Jewish couple, both of whom said they were offended by the service. When we told the groom, he said he sat us between them on purpose and thought it was hilarious. When I told the bishop what had happened, he said, "If both sides were angry, you know you did a good job."

A good friend tells a funny story about being invited to be the godfather to the child of his best friends. The minister who was to officiate informed the child's mother that my friend wasn't able to be a godfather because he wasn't a member of their denomination. However, the mother had done her homework and informed the priest that the rules state only one of the godparents need be of their denomination. He begrudgingly relented. After the service when it came time for the godparents to sign the baptismal registry, the priest slammed the book shut before my friend could sign it. After they left the church, the mother said, "I didn't bother to tell him you were gay."

Unfortunately, some of the most uncomfortable experiences I have had have been when families have asked me to participate in the funeral of their loved one. Of course, you want to be respectful of another person's tradition, but in all fairness there are often mixed messages. People of other faiths and denominations are often not sure what to do, especially at Communion time, such as the time I was invited to preach at my Uncle Charles's funeral. The priest walked toward me with the chalice, and as I reached for it, he pulled it away, nodded at me, thanked me for understanding, and walked away.

I spent a lot of time with Brad Rock, his wife Franny, and their four young sons while Brad was dying of cancer. Brad fought bravely, but when it became apparent the chemotherapy wasn't working, he handled the situation with his family thoughtfully and directly. His often-used phrase was "It is what it is." Then he'd fix a martini and smoke a cigar.

Franny asked me if I would preach at his memorial service. I said, "Of course, I would be honored." I received a lovely invitation to preach from the president of the parochial school his boys attended. Unfortunately, the day of the service, the president was not able to attend. When I walked in the door of the church with my vestments, the officiant asked, "Who are you?" When I explained, he said, "Well, you cannot preach." I then showed him my name in the program and told him he would have to explain to the widow and over a thousand mourners why I was there and wasn't preaching.

He relented. But he told me I could not sit anywhere near the altar and could not receive Communion, and pointed to a chair in the corner.

Outraged by the way I had been treated, Franny made sure that at the reception following the service, the first thing I got was a martini. I needed it. I understand the president of the institution was not pleased about the way I had been treated. Soon after, I heard the priest was reassigned.

I attended a memorial service for a friend's father at a convent school in Washington, DC, where I had often attended services. Following the service, the celebrant asked to speak to me. The son of the man for whom the service was said glared at the priest and replied, "No, you may *not* speak to him!" He realized the celebrant did not approve of my receiving communion. I guess my Anglican collar was a giveaway. Had I known it was going to create such a scene, I would have stayed seated during Communion. Later that day I heard from the Mother Superior, who apologized, invited me to come back anytime, and said she would never invite that particular priest to celebrate again.

However, miracles do happen. When Lacey O'Donnell and J. P. Matan married in Rehoboth Beach in the middle a hurricane, the Roman Catholic priest got stuck in traffic due to the closure of the Chesapeake Bay Bridge. I received a special dispensation to administer Communion!

I have to say, Episcopal clergy can be difficult and territorial as well, and that was a big lesson to me early on. Just after I was ordained, an elderly friend of the family who was terminally ill asked if I would come to give her Communion using the 1928 Book of Common Prayer. My dad flew me out to Seattle, and I was honored to oblige—that is until the following Sunday, when I was upbraided by the rector of her church for my using the 1928 book, as he had had a difficult time introducing the 1979 book to his congregation. The truth is, I would do it again.

BEATS THE ALTERNATIVE?
One day in a discussion with Ruth Johnson about the dangers of aggressive medical treatment, I said, "Beats the alternative."

Ruth said, "Will, I thought you were supposed to tell me the exact opposite."

Legacy

I HAVE A PAINTING AT HOME GIVEN TO ME BY MARIAN SMITH MILLER. It is by the great African-American primitive artist, Sister Gertrude Morgan. She painted it on a box top. Sister Gertrude sits on Jesus's lap in her wedding dress. Jesus is wearing a tuxedo. Like me, he has red hair. We may never know what Jesus looked like, but according to Sister Gertrude and Marian, he looked like me.

I think that's probably as close as I'll come to being like Jesus.

I have just recently seen the actress Bette Midler starring in *Hello, Dolly!* at the Shubert Theatre on Broadway. I was struck by something written in the "Who's Who in the Cast." It said of Ms. Midler that "she would like to offer her profound thanks to the creators of this production and to let everyone know that it is a privilege and an honor to share the stage with this brilliant and talented company."

Thankfully, at this point in my life, I have come to understand that my life really isn't just about me. It's about the ensemble, and I can look back now and see I had some lessons to learn.

As I said in an earlier chapter, as a young man pursuing a musical theater career, I was so absorbed with perfecting my own performance that I was missing out on what now means the most to me about life. While playing Cornelius Hackl, I'm not so sure I cared so much about Barnaby or Minnie or one of the dancers in "The Waiters' Gallop." I waited for the thundering applause singling me out over the others. I have to confess it is still somewhat of a temptation, particularly after delivering a sermon. At this point, a thumbs-up from just one of the kids suits me just fine.

Being a priest has me performing with a different sort of ensemble. Curiously, it has involved every element of the theater without my realizing it. Church is musical theater. But the actors are all in real-life roles, and someday the show will go on even without me.

For me, every scene is performed with the backdrop being a cross. As a symbol I find it very realistic. There is no pretending what is in store for us. It is a symbol of death to be sure, but it is also a symbol of love, forgiveness, and hope.

When choosing photographs for this book, I didn't have pictures of many of the folks about whom you have read, many of whom are now gone, but their faces and the roles they played are emblazoned in my mind and heart.

Before the final curtain, I am honored to hold hands with the entire cast and take our bow together.

The Final Curtain

The secret of a good sermon is to have a good beginning and a good ending, and having the two as close together as possible.
—George Burns

When I was walking down the hall at ES-LA this week, I realized my shoes were loose and I was shuffling. I started laughing to myself. It made me think of Emma Hagedorn. At about eighty, she was a devoted member of Sargent House at St. Columba's. Emma was very tall and thin, and her shoes never fit. She was the sweetest person and shuffled everywhere she went. You could always hear her coming and going, carrying sandwiches, cookies, tea, or lemonade.

One day when we sat down for lunch, someone said, "Where's Emma?" Craig Eder answered, "She's under the table." Of course, everyone started laughing hysterically because he meant his dog Emma, who always came with him and would lie at his feet.

Thinking back, what I remember best about Sargent House is the laughter coming from the lunch table or the Bible study.

And, you know what I hope? I hope that when the time comes for me to die—or "shuffle off," as Peg Rueckert would say—I will again hear the laughter from the folks from Sargent House. I will again see Craig, Emma, and Esther with her poultice.

The gang from St. Mark's will be there. Jean will be there doing the little "di do" she did bringing up the collection plates, and Bill will be in the choir urging me to hurry it up to get to tee time. Marjorie and Ned will be there in the front pew, Ned snoring.

The St. Albans contingent will be well represented. Pete, Jack, Ben, Katie, and Willis. John Selinger yelling at Eddie, Billy, and Adrien to "tuck in your shirts!"

Hopefully Herb Gronauer will introduce me to Frank Sinatra and Bob Hope.

Marian will ask, "What took you so long?"

Dad will be surprised he's there, and George will be in his three-piece suit.

Mom will be there reminding me, "That's enough now, honey."